Spiritual Di[rection]
in the Footsteps of
the Shepherd

Mother Nadine

Intercessors of the Lamb
Omaha, NE

Additional copies of this book may be obtained through our online store or by contacting:

Intercessors of the Lamb

11811 Calhoun Road
Omaha, NE 68152

e-mail: bellwether@novia.net
web site: www.bellwetheromaha.org

Published in the United States.

ISBN: 0-9664956-7-5

Spiritual Direction in the Footsteps of the Shepherd

Chapter 1

Introduction – Only Two Paths

"Enter through the narrow gate, for the gate is wide and the road broad that leads to destruction and those who enter through it are many" (Mt 7:13-14).

> *"Spiritual direction is an invitation to grow."*

What is spiritual direction? Though not everyone is called to be a spiritual director, hopefully we are all directees so we have an idea of what a spiritual director expects of a person under spiritual direction.

Spiritual direction, in general, is really an invitation to grow. It is not a command. We are free to accept that invitation or reject it. God is still going to love us if we refuse. He will still love us. He **is** love. Yet, there are only two paths, and it is our choice, one or the other. One leads toward heaven and the other toward hell. That is a tremendous reality.

I hadn't thought a lot about hell in my lifetime. I knew it to be a reality. I knew it was in Scripture and is mentioned a few times in the gospels. But it wasn't really until I was doing some deliverance ministry one day that the Lord put it upon my heart to call forth the Judas spirit. Now a priest had called me several months ago and asked if I'd ever run into that particular spirit and I said, "No". I think deep in my heart I never really thought Judas was in hell. The Church doesn't really teach it. Jesus just said, "It would be better had he not been born" (Mt 26:24). But I called forth this spirit and the Lord said to call forth the spirit of damnation. That is when the deliverance was done – big time. I began to realize that Judas has a lot to do with this spirit of damnation. I am not here to say with certainty that Judas is in hell. That is up to the Church to say for sure where he is but I tell you, the reality of hell really came to me at that time.

You will find this to be true particularly when you are doing deliverance ministry. You will find people who are having a terrible experience of what hell is like; they are almost going through it within themselves. So when our theologians and people who are experts in spiritual direction tell us, "There are only two paths," we must remember that Jesus said it too. There are only the two kingdoms; you are with Him or you are not. You will find that people will be on one path or the other. It is like the narrow gate. In Matthew 7:13-14, Jesus said, "Enter through the narrow gate, for the gate is wide and the road broad that leads to destruction and those who enter through it are many." I do not think I ever heard Jesus' words as clearly as I did in this context. He said, "How narrow the gate and constricted the road that leads to life and those who find it are few." That is quite sobering isn't it? Those who find it are few. These are the words of Jesus.

Our time here on earth is short. There is a great need for spiritual direction, so that the people of God are not left wandering around for ever and ever in rebellion and disobedience. We all know that when the Israelites were called out of Egypt, it took them forty years to get into the Promised Land. The Promised Land for us is that union with God. It took the Israelites forty years to make it. Yet, we know that they could have made it in three days. It was only a three day journey. Isn't that sad? How badly we do need spiritual direction and spiritual directors in our lives!

Chapter 2

The Need for Spiritual Direction

"He who trusts in himself is a fool" (Prov 28:26).

> *"God is placing within the hearts of His people a deep hunger and thirst for Him."*

There is a real hunger and thirst in people. We are seeing a tremendous change here as we travel lately. We are seeing a tremendous change in the things that we hear and in the letters that we receive. There is a deep, deep hunger for God, so this is a very fruitful time. In other words, the harvest is very, very ripe. God is placing within the hearts of His people, and within our own hearts as well, a deep hunger and thirst for Him, a deep desire to know Him in a very intimate way – not just to obey laws and precepts. That is not what He is after. He wants a personal relationship.

To have that, we need a guide. Scripture says, "He who trusts in himself [or directs himself] is a fool" (Prov 28:26). We take that very seriously. We need a guide. Father Dubay says that we need someone to speak to us of God, someone who already knows God and who has God overflowing in their hearts, who has the light and love of the Holy Spirit. In other words, we also need a co-discerner. We are far too close to ourselves to discern anything very well. A spiritual director will definitely help us to discern. A spiritual director will help us to detect the movement of the Holy Spirit in our life and, if we are spiritual directors, detect the movement of the Spirit in others' lives. We are not totally objective. We think we are. We think we are detached until somebody does not return our favorite pen. It could be the tiniest thing. We think we are detached until we find somebody sitting in our place at Church, "Well, that is my place you know!" The Holy Spirit has all sorts of ways of letting us know where our attachments are. We are just not totally objective in discerning our own life situations.

St. Ignatius of Loyola, in his rules for discernment, says, "For good discernment, we must be disinterested." Well, it is pretty hard to get disinterested in oneself. That rationale can click in and say, "Oh, yes, I am in neutral," until... .

So, we do need someone else. We need somebody who is impartial. That is why, as we discern so many of the requests that come into Bellwether, it is not too difficult for us since we have no personal knowledge or interest in the situations for which we pray. We do not even know most of the people who ask us for prayers. We are disinterested, but when you do know your directee, it takes discipline to be disinterested. By disinterested we do not mean that we are not interested in the person, himself. Rather, it means that we are more interested in the movement of the Spirit

11

within him because we want to keep him on the safe path. So a spiritual director helps us to be more objective, more outside of ourselves and helps us to get to Jesus, and not by our own way but by His way. A spiritual director will also help us to reassess our life situations – how we are dealing with our jobs or with the culture in which we live.

"Spiritual direction concerns the movement of the Spirit within."

Spiritual direction is different than confession. Some priests who are confessors are also spiritual directors, but we are seeing that less and less now. Other people are directing more now. A spiritual director takes in the whole person. Are you rested? Are you eating right? What are your feelings? What are your activities? Who are you associating with? All these things are important. You want to bring everything to spiritual direction.

There is something in our nature that wants to share. We want to share our times of joy with someone who can understand the movement of the Spirit within. We want to share our periods of trauma, our pain. That is how God made us. He did not make us to walk the walk alone or to make the journey alone.

To be a directee, we need the desire to grow in relationship with the Lord. We need to be willing to put forth the effort into that. If you are a spiritual director and somebody is coming to you who does not have that desire for a relationship with the Lord, or who does not want to make the time needed for that commitment, then they are probably not ready for spiritual direction. There really isn't anything to direct, is there?

Spiritual direction concerns the movement of the Spirit within. The Holy Spirit acts within a person, within their human spirit. It takes discernment to understand His movements. It takes a lot of discernment. The most difficult discernment is to distinguish between the movement and the action of the Holy Spirit and the action of the human spirit. We have to be careful in the early stages of the person's walk that we do not keep saying to the directee, "That is your spirit. That is your spirit." We always have to affirm them. As they start to grow they will begin to see more and more, "Oh that was me." The Spirit is going to start letting them know.

Thomas Merton says that "Spiritual direction is a continual process of formation and guidance in which a Christian is led and encouraged in his special vocation, whether it is to the single life, married life or religious life, that by faithful

> *"God made us to desire to share our lives...not to walk the walk alone.."*

correspondence to the graces of the Holy Spirit, he may attain to the particular end of his vocation and to union with God." That is what we want to do. We always want to help a person live out that particular state of life to which God has called them, leading them to union with Him. Father Rossage directed me on my thirty-day discernment retreat. This is what he says about spiritual direction: "It is a process in which one person (that is the directee) meets with another competent person (who is, of course, the director) in order to seek some guidance, reassurance, discernment and affirmation in developing a deeper relationship with the Lord."

Being competent does not mean that you have to know a lot intellectually, although you do need to know basic teachings of the Church. It helps to know how the saints were led. But I think, for us, competent means especially and maybe first of all, does that person pray? Do I have a spiritual director who prays, who can even pick up the Holy Spirit? In other words, does he know the Holy Spirit? This is what we are always after. There are three parties in spiritual direction. The director and the directee listen and learn from their conversation with the other. The third party is the Holy Spirit. He is the most important person of all.

Spiritual direction is an ongoing conversation – a personal encounter – between the director and the directee. Spiritual direction is initiated by the directee. Spiritual directors do not call them up and say, "Hey, I haven't seen you in a month." We leave them free. If they come and they want an appointment, fine. But it must be initiated by the directee for the purpose of growing in a life of faith. The director enters into this invitation of the directee only to facilitate the growth and the development of that directee. If the directee is not initiating the contact, it means that he is not ready or is taking it casually or perhaps that the timing is wrong. Oftentimes it means that the person is not praying so there is nothing to direct. It can be many things. But the point is, the directee must initiate the direction.

The growth and the development of the directee is the highest priority. This, too, is determined by the directees themselves in prayer, in reflection, and in relationship with God. In other words, if they want to pray, if they are journaling, if they have something to direct, you know their heart is in the right place and that there is some kind of growth going on. But the growth will be in proportion to their disciplines and how much they really want to be directed.

There are a few things that spiritual direction is not. It is not psychological counseling. It is not psychotherapy. I mention that because we live in a culture today where therapy seems to be the trend. When I came home from the cloister and started offering spiritual direction, it was reported right away to the Chancery: "Oh, she is doing spiritual direction and she does not have a degree in counseling." Isn't it interesting how people associate spiritual direction with therapy? I asked the Archbishop, "Do you want me to go to Creighton University to get a degree in counseling or in anything psychological?" He said, "No. I'll never stop anyone from praying and you pray." He let me continue. So be careful that you are not becoming a psychologist or strictly a counselor. Spiritual directors get to know a lot about temperaments, we get to know a lot about different things, but we are not counselors with degrees.

Spiritual direction is not friends getting together to share the Lord. That is a wonderful thing. We are not saying that you should not get together with friends to share the Lord. But that is not spiritual direction. Spiritual direction is not for those seeking information just to help them in their spiritual growth. This is the mind taking precedence over the heart and curiosity is not a virtue, really. Spiritual direction is not shared insights even in small groups. You want these insights. You want to see what other people are hearing from the Lord. It will help us in our discernment, but it is not a spiritual direction session.

Also, direction, for most of us, is not the time for the Sacrament of Reconciliation. You might have a spiritual director who is a priest and who will combine confession and spiritual direction. Many times in the Church, spiritual direction took place in the confessional, because the confessor was an excellent spiritual director and it may have been the only time he had. I am not saying that it cannot be combined, but it is not the same. The Sacrament of Reconciliation compliments spiritual direction. Whereas the Sacrament forgives our sins and strengthens us against future temptations, spiritual direction tries to get to the root of these sins and addresses what we are going to do about it. It will challenge us to change so that we can grow.

Chapter 3

What Is a Spiritual Director?

"May the God of peace himself make you perfectly holy
and may you entirely, spirit, soul, and body, be preserved
blameless for the coming of our Lord Jesus Christ"
(1 Thes 5:23).

"The role of the director is to
listen and to support."

The term spiritual director can be misleading because
spiritual direction really takes into account the whole
person. St. Paul said, "May the God of peace himself make
you perfectly holy and may you entirely, spirit, soul, and
body, be preserved blameless for the coming of our Lord
Jesus Christ." (1 Thes 5:23). Paul talks about body, soul
and spirit. He is talking about the whole person. Spiritual
direction is concerned with the whole person. It should
address that person's needs, concerns and sinful areas. It
should address all that the person is thinking and living,
their fears and whatever they want to bring. If you are the
directee, everything about yourself can be brought to the

17

director because we should relate to the Lord with our entire being and not just with this little part or that little part. We cannot separate our spirituality into parts. Spiritual direction is for that wholeness.

Oftentimes people think when they hear the term "spiritual director," it implies some kind of authority. I have heard this many times: "Well my spiritual director says," as if it were a sin that a director's advice not be followed. It is important to remember that a spiritual director does not have authority. The director cannot order the directee to do anything. It is very important that you know that and remember that. The spiritual director can suggest and, like God does, invite. He can point out the better choice, the more perfect way, but a spiritual director cannot insist that a person do that.

The role of the director is to listen, to support and as I said, sometimes to be a co-discerner, to help the directee discern the Lord's will for them. The focus of spiritual direction is always to further one's relationship with the Lord. In order to do that, it does require regular meetings – regular meetings and a one to one relationship. Spiritual direction is not done in a group setting and ideally is a face to face meeting. Directors have to be very careful not to impose or even try to impose their own ideas or their own spirituality on the one they are directing. Again, the spiritual director really has to shift into neutral and become disinterested so that his own self is out of it and he is really trying to pick up the way the Spirit is leading the directee. I have been directing for quite a while and I have never seen the Holy Spirit direct two people the same way, ever.

We have to be very intent on what He wants to do, and we never know what the Holy Spirit wants to do. As retreat directors, when we give retreats, usually during the first couple of days, we do not yet know the direction of the Spirit. We have to kind of throw this out and throw that out and in about 24 to 48 hours, we begin to see, way before the retreatant is seeing it, the direction of the Spirit. We are going to see things before the directee does, but we have to wait until they catch up with us. We have to see it almost before they do or we cannot direct them. We always have to be at least one step ahead if possible, so that we can direct.

Being a spiritual director is a calling. It is a call upon our hearts. Spiritual writers tell us that many times, the spiritual director is the last one to even think that he is called to this ministry, but there are some things you might look for. The Holy Spirit will be working in the person who is seeking a director because the Holy Spirit is the director of souls and He wants flesh and blood representation. He will gently move that person. If you find that somebody starts coming up to you and asking you questions, things about their life or sharing, they are probably being drawn to you by the Holy Spirit. Oftentimes that is the way the Holy Spirit will say to you, "I want you to be My visible representative here. I will direct you so you can direct them."

> *"The focus of spiritual direction is always to further one's relationship with the Lord."*

We are called simply to collaborate with God. Paul says, "For we are God's co-workers" (1 Cor 3:9). Isn't that beautiful? This is how we work with God. We work to pick up the Holy Spirit. Spiritual directors sometimes have to beg for that grace, "Help me pick You up!" We have to do a lot of intercession for the people that we direct. We cannot function like passive mechanical instruments. In our prayer life we have to be sure we are picking up the Holy Spirit ourselves.

We do not want to do anything to frustrate God's work or to block Him from reaching a person. It is amazing to see a person receive confirmation from the Lord. When they begin to hear, "This is the way; walk in it," how free they become! Oftentimes, deep in their hearts, they begin to perceive something. They just need us to confirm. We don't tell them but we are definitely there to confirm – which is one of the basic rules of the Holy Spirit. So if others are seeking you out for direction, then in all humility, seek God and really say, "Am I the one now to help them, because they seem to be seeking me out?" That is usually a pretty good sign. A spiritual director must always be deeply aware of his own personal inadequacy because he always needs that element of humility to be directed himself, to be docile to the leading of the Spirit.

Spiritual directors are not limited to priests and religious. For some time in the Church we thought that a spiritual director must be a priest or a religious, but the times have changed a great, great deal. The gift is given to priests; it is given to religious but it does not come automatically because a person is a priest or religious. So, just because you might go to a certain religious or priest, do not automatically think that he or she is a good spiritual director or that they have the gift of spiritual direction. Seek God's mind, His counsel and He will usually lead you to the person He wants to direct you so that He, Himself, can direct you. He may just have your paths cross – and you know. If you find that it does not work for you, then always feel free to find another one. You have to be able to trust that person and have a rapport with that person. But the Holy Spirit has His way of putting people in contact with other people when he wants it. You just kind of know. It takes prayer. Spiritual directors are few and far between in the Church. This is why we want to start training spiritual directors here and now.

It is not to be taken lightly. St. John of the Cross says this, "There is almost an infinite gain in being right and an infinite loss in being wrong" (see *The Fire Within*, Fr. Thomas Dubay, p. 295). I hope you heard that. You cannot afford to miss. You cannot miss. You could do so much damage to a person who is trusting that when you speak, they think it is the Lord. You must make sure it is. If you find that you are not sure, simply say, "I do not know. Let's keep discerning. Let me pray about it more."

Chapter 4

The Purpose of Spiritual Direction

"...that they may be one as we are" (Jn 17:11).

> *"The centerpiece of spiritual direction is to speak the truth in love."*

The purpose of spiritual direction is to try to get beneath the surface of a person's life. Most of our interactions with people, are "superficial" aren't they? We can wear many hats, so to speak. Do not do that with a spiritual director. Spiritual directors want to get behind the façade of conventional attitudes and gestures that a person may present to the world. Perhaps the person has to for different reasons, but when you are together there is a friendship that develops. You become a soul companion in a sense, somebody that is walking a very deep, intimate journey with another. This will bring out within the directee an inner spiritual freedom so that he can feel safe in your presence. He must know that he can say whatever he needs to say, knowing you are not judging him at any time.

Fr. Thomas Dubay once said that "The Church should aim at making saints, nothing less" (*Seeking Spiritual Direction*). This is also the goal of spiritual direction. You want to go for transforming union. You want to go to the maximum. You want to challenge, to help that person live the Gospel and come into a very deep, deep union with God. Try to recognize God's presence in all of his activities so he can start to see that movement of God as much as you can. You will be able to see and say, "Oh, there is the Lord there," or "Did you see that gift here?" You are constantly building him up and helping him to become aware of the movement of God in his life, not just in his prayer life or journal but in all the events of his life as well.

Another purpose of spiritual direction or discernment is simply the dialogue and this is good. It is good to have someone in whose presence we can just let it all hang out, where we can just be. We do not have to be right. We do not have to be wrong. Nothing is judged. The directee must feel free enough to say, "This is how I am feeling. This is how I reacted. This is it. What do I do now? Help me. Help me on the journey."

You will begin to see, in a powerful way, where people are on the journey. Some will be beginners. You have to see where they are. They are not into contemplation at that stage, so do not expect it of them. They are in a meditation type of prayer. It is totally different. We have people coming to our center all the time who have never even heard of journaling and who really do not pray, but they **are** coming. So we back up to the basics, the ABC's. You will find many people who are in the Illuminative Way. You are going to see that their spiritual life is quite different. Direction for them changes a little bit then. When you find people in the Unitive Way, it changes a great deal. If a person is in the Dark Night, you learn how to direct there. You will be able to spot the different levels but you have to know where they are. **They** do not have to know, and this is why we do not emphasize the seven mansions of Teresa of Avila too much anymore. People got all bent out of shape trying to determine which mansion they were in. God wasn't even part of the prayer anymore; it became "all about me." Often, though, a person may not know where he is; it is a good thing because it takes his focus off himself. We want him to focus on God but **we** need to know where he is. We cannot direct a person if we do not have a good idea of where he is; and if we do not know where a person is, we have to go to God and ask Him, "Lord, show me what I need to know. I need more light on this particular situation."

The centerpiece of spiritual direction is to speak the truth in love. Do not hedge on truth, ever. You will be out of the Holy Spirit. He is the Spirit of truth. That is why the truth can set us free (Jn 8:32). Do not hedge. Do not think to yourself, "Oh, I don't know how to say this. They think this is all the Holy Spirit here." Maybe it is really a mixture. You must be very careful. Ask the Lord for wisdom, prudence, and the right timing. Ask Him how He wants you to point it out. But remember, the centerpiece of good spiritual direction is to speak the truth but in love.

The development of spiritual direction is very interesting. Spiritual direction officially was instituted in the 6th century. It came out of a need to revive the spiritual life of monks and people whose religious life had fallen into disarray. Well, look at the Church today! Perhaps this is why spiritual direction is getting more popular and is so desperately needed. Bishops and abbots back then saw that the current practices of penance, confession and absolution provided inadequate means of redirecting the life of the penitent. Isn't that interesting? I think we have all experienced that; you can go to confession every day if you want and say the same thing. That confession alone may not challenge you or change you. You may begin to think that you do not have to change but can just keep going back for the same thing. The church Fathers started to pick this up in the sixth century – that the Sacrament itself was not changing people enough. I thought that was very interesting! They needed to have direction. The renewal and reformation of one's moral character remained incomplete. Penitents just were not changing.

Spiritual direction goes beyond forgiveness. God always forgives us, but we have to deal with how we are forgiving as well. What are we going to do about it? What are we going to do about these thoughts? A lot of this can get tremendous help in spiritual direction because a director can give us some practical tools and methods to avoid repetition of the same sin, and we always need more tools.

> *"Fr. Thomas Dubay once said that 'The Church should aim at making saints, nothing less.'"*

In the middle of the 20th century, spiritual direction got another kind of a face. This is where psychology, psychoanalysis and psychotherapy became the primary way of alleviating mental and emotional disorders. This began to take over in place of spiritual direction. But then, people began to realize that it was ineffective. People began to notice that it was not really changing them. It was not enough. So an interest

25

during the mid-20th century in spirituality and spiritual direction began to grow and this is what the Church came up with. The Catholic Church and many other Christian denominations were ill-prepared to keep up with the demand. People started to realize that psychology and psychiatry were not enough. They realized, "I need more."

This is where we are now. We are beginning to see that we need more healing at the very root of our being, in our spirit; this is what needs the ministry. Immediately following Vatican II and up to the 1970s, gifted trainers (directors) and new schools of spiritual direction evolved. The former severe modes yielded to another style of direction in which the director put his personal experience at the service of the directee. We need experience. But we must be careful that we do not deny the directee's experience of the Holy Spirit simply because their experience differs from ours. We have to leave the Spirit free and as you direct, you will find there are many experiences people have that you have not had. That is just fine. Your main experience has to be of the Holy Spirit Himself and how diverse He is! Yet, He can bring about unity. How each soul is incredibly different!

Chapter 5

Spiritual Direction Today

"For where two or three are gathered together in my name, there am I in the midst of them" (Mt 18:20).

> *"As a rule, in spiritual direction, if we do not move forward, we will regress."*

We are living in a time now of a new discovery and interest in spiritual direction. We have heard a lot about centering prayer because it began to be rediscovered as people started praying. But now we also know there is a false centering prayer. False centering prayer teaches that if a person does this and this and this to become centered, then God is going to come and something is going to happen. That is not authentic centering prayer. There is authentic centering prayer that Teresa of Avila talks about, which is led by the Lord. When you are directing someone, you are going to know when God has led them into authentic centering prayer. Then you can affirm them there.

An article on spiritual direction said that what we revived today in our spiritual direction is the ancient Christian ministry of healing. Isn't that beautiful? Evidently in the early Church there was a lot of healing taking place in spiritual direction and there is a lot of healing that takes place in spiritual direction today too.

Spiritual directors place much more emphasis today on the role of Scripture in prayer rather than simply telling a directee to read a certain book. There is nothing wrong with spiritual reading but now we direct people much more with the words of Jesus rather than formal spiritual reading. We are living in a wonderful age, where we live much more out of the word of God Himself and out of the Gospel.

As I said previously, the lived experience of directors will have a great deal to do with direction. For example, it will help if you, out of your own experience – whatever it is, (your directees do not have to know what your experiences are) – can help someone become much more compassionate and more patient, particularly if you have been in similar situations. It does not have to be in the exact situation; but if you have been in pain, if you have been rejected, if you have been lonely, that will all come into your direction because it is a part of you. You will bring so much of your heart into your spiritual direction.

One of the benefits of being in spiritual direction is that, as we walk this walk with our director, we are maturing because we ourselves are growing. We are

> *"We will never reach the end here. There is always room for growth."*

growing in our relationship with God. As we grow in that relationship, we definitely grow in discernment because we begin to get more light and we start to see the light and the darkness. I need to see the darkness within myself, first and foremost, before I begin to see it in the enemy or in anybody else. We start to say, "Oh I did not know I had this. I did not know this had to go. I did not know that was attached there. My goodness Lord, I did not know this." We did not know but we are aware now. We did not know but now we are getting light and it is wonderful. A good director is going to affirm you in any kind of light. And if you are a spiritual director you want to be sure you affirm, affirm, affirm as much as you can and challenge the directee always to grow further. We will never reach the end here. There is always room for growth. In the spiritual life remember that if we do not move forward, we cannot tread water very long. As a rule, in spiritual direction, if we do not move forward, we will regress. It is like mountain climbing. It is a slow methodical climb. You might stop to rest, but if you rest too long, you start to slide back. So we want to make sure that we see constant growth more and more, and grow deeper and deeper in union.

What is the difference between those who seek spiritual direction and those who are actually ready for it? You need to know this. There is a difference between those who seek and those who are really ready for it. There are many questions you need to ask the potential directee. If you are the one seeking spiritual direction, ask yourself, "What are my expectations in seeking spiritual direction? What is my motive? What precisely do I wish to gain through spiritual direction?" That's going to tell you a lot.

The four requirements for spiritual direction are:
  1) The person must have the desire to grow in deeper relationship with the Lord.

2) The person must have a consistent prayer life.
3) The person should be keeping a journal of regular prayer experiences as much as possible.
4) The person must be willing to meet regularly with a director in order to form a consistent relationship.

Those are important points to remember. Oftentimes we find that after people get started, they do not call. They are not praying. Then it may be two, three months and all of a sudden there is a crisis or something and the phone rings. These people are not ready for spiritual direction because there basically is nothing to direct. You have to have a relationship, somehow, with the director himself. A person must truly want to grow. If he does not want to grow, then he is content at being self-directed with no accountability; and if we do not have accountability to anybody in our prayer life, we will start to slide back. That is the child within us. The child within us needs accountability. There is a lot of self-help on the market today. You can learn guitar all by yourself; you can learn piano or now just keyboard. But have you ever noticed that if you are left on your own, you skip a lesson here, you skip something there? There is no teacher; there is no one to whom I have to be accountable. It is the same with spiritual direction. It all comes out of relationship. Remember to keep your own prayer life under accountability.

> *"We pray with our directees."*

We do not share everything we know with our directees until we know how to pray with them and until they arrive there themselves. We do not want to say to a directee, "God said... ." If you do that you will strip them of the freedom they need for that beautiful part of their journey.

We pray with our directees. Your prayer should rest on what you are getting from the Lord at that moment. You will not have a team because spiritual direction is very confidential. Directees must be able to trust their directors. If you are a director, you need to be trustworthy of their confidences. You have to be sure when you are praying with your directee, that you are picking up the Lord. If you are not, you have to have the gift of prudence to know what to share and what not to share because your directee is very vulnerable; that person is wide open. There is no defense there. That is why you have to be very careful.

Do not be overwhelmed. We discern more than we think. As we hear about people's journeys, we will pick up things right away. We will be able to identify the movement of the Spirit. You can then pray that they begin to pick up His movement, and when they do, you confirm them.

Chapter 6

The Role of the Spiritual Director

"He must increase; I must decrease" (Jn 3:30).

---

*"The ideal role model
for a spiritual director
is John the Baptist."*

The primary role of the spiritual director is to help the directee work toward holiness. We directors always have to work toward holiness ourselves. Thomas Merton said that the first duty of the spiritual director if he wants to be an effective director is to see to his own interior life and take time for prayer and meditation, since he will never be able to give to others what he does not possess himself. Sounds familiar, doesn't it? We cannot give to others what we do not have ourselves. So both the director and the directee are working to become holy and to remove sin and attachments.

Spiritual pride is found especially in those who direct others. Isn't that interesting? I am taking these notes from a lot of theologians and people in the Church, as well as a lot of the saints who have done direction. Spiritual pride is especially found in those who direct others. So directors need to be watchful for spiritual pride; it can lead to false mysticism. Many times in our Church today, we are directing people who are definitely into false mysticism themselves. If we are into false mysticism through pride, we will become the blind leading the blind. We are definitely seeing this happen today. The best remedy for spiritual pride is deep humility. Pray for it; it is a gift; it is grace. Pray for it, and then accept it in whatever work God wants to give us. He does listen to our prayer.

The ideal role model for a spiritual director is John the Baptist. Isn't that wonderful! We are so close to him; he is so close to this call. Theologians tell us that he makes the ideal role model because John had a deep experience of God in his own life. He definitely had a call from God and he had the humility to focus always on

> *"A spiritual director is one loving soul setting another on fire."*

Jesus and to point to Jesus. Remember, John said, "He must increase; I must decrease" (Jn 3:30). These are such simple little words, but they are the basis of humility. One interesting translation of that same Scripture verse is, "He must increase, and I must disappear." That is what God is calling us to do. John said, "Look! There is the Lamb of God." A spiritual director is always pointing one to Jesus. John the Baptist had a great peace and joy in doing that. Spiritual directors have a great peace and joy in seeing the directee grow in their spiritual life. You might even see them bypassing you, but there still remains a peace and joy knowing that God used you to help them on their way.

John did not insist on his own ideas or his own expectations. He was very brief. He said only what needed to be said. He did not need a lot of extra words. Sometimes, those of us in spiritual direction can get pretty wordy. We can get excited when we see somebody get a light and we can start thinking, "Oh my! I remember when I got that light!" All of a sudden we are talking more about ourselves than about the directee. I used to do this a lot more than I do today. I still do it sometimes. One time a directee said, "You know, could you listen to me for a while." I realized then that the lights God gave me were for me and the lights God gives a directee are for them. We have to be very careful to be brief and to be much more interested in what God is doing in their life.

> *"The Holy Spirit knows our directee far better than we do."*

In John 3:29, John the Baptist says, "The one who has the bride, is the bridegroom." He is speaking of Jesus. "The best man who stands and listens rejoices greatly at the bride groom's voice. Then, this joy of mine has been made complete." This is how a director feels when that grace comes. Our role today is similar.

Specialists in this field tell us that the holier a director becomes himself, the gentler he also becomes. The director becomes less scandalized over people's faults, because he understands man's weakened condition much, much better, particularly if he has walked the walk. It might not be the same identical walk; it might not be the same identical manifestation of sin; it might not be the same type of suffering, but compassion goes a long way when you have been there. You can certainly understand somebody else and you become very gentle, very non-judgmental. St. Augustine says that it is one loving soul setting another on fire. Isn't that beautiful? That is what spiritual direction is. A spiritual director is one loving soul setting another on fire. A spiritual director is a co-discerner and helps interpret the Holy Spirit. A spiritual director is someone who is walking the journey with a person. The person is not alone. The journey is shared and the Holy Spirit leads at all times. Director and directee actually assist the Holy Spirit.

It is important to remember that the spiritual director also is being led. He must be a follower. He has a tremendous responsibility to allow the Spirit to lead so that through the Holy Spirit, he may be God's mouthpiece and lead another. There really is no special formula. Simply follow the Holy Spirit. Docility to the Holy Spirit is key. A spiritual director prays a lot for his directees. "Holy Spirit, give me the wisdom; let me hear what You want me to hear. Let me say what You want to say. Let me be Your instrument, Your mouthpiece." This is extremely important for our personal relationship with the Holy Spirit to remain intact.

> *"Learn to wait upon the Lord."*

There isn't any one way that is best for all because the Holy Spirit is very diverse, and unique. The Holy Spirit knows that person far better than we do. So we have to be careful that we do not teach our way or from our experience, that we do not determine what is the best way for a directee to pray. We just have to pick up the leading of the Holy Spirit; we learn to listen to the directee's heart. Many times a person will say one thing but his heart is saying something else. You learn to listen to the heart.

We need to lead souls in God's way and not our own way. A spiritual director helps another recognize the Lord's leading. It is not enough that we simply pick it up ourselves. We must always try to impart that to the directee. We must always be thinking, "This is what I sense is the leading of the Lord. This is how he led before." You will start to see a pattern. Point that pattern

> "This is extremely important work. It is very sacred work to walk this journey with a soul, very sacred. It is the work of a soul; it is the work of the Spirit; it is very holy."

out. Because you can see it, you can be more objective. If you cannot see it, ask the Holy Spirit to begin to show you the way He is leading your directee and then simply follow the inspirations of grace that he is getting. We want to be able to reach the Lord with them. We do not want to reach the Lord ourselves and then say, "Hey! I am here! Come on up," or "Let's get our act together." Help them walk the walk; stay with them all the way. So it takes a little patience – sometimes a lot of patience – for them to cooperate with the movement of the Spirit and that comes through prayer. I think one of the reasons that spiritual direction is a wonderful ministry for intercessors is because intercessors already pray. We already pray for God's people. We are the discerners; we are usually the intercessors for those we are directing as well, whether on a regular basis or for retreat work.

Thomas Merton says that the director's function is to verify and encourage what is truly spiritual in the soul. Look for what is spiritual and point that out. Point out what is natural and the direction in which you see God calling that person.

Because a spiritual director becomes a co-discerner, we teach directees to distinguish between good and evil tendencies to help them follow through on the good fruit. Sometimes they want to know about a decision. Help them map that out. "Let's say we make this decision. Where will you be with that in two weeks, a month? Is that going to be the kind of fruit you want?" Walk it through; help them. Work it through with them so that they can arrive at the end to which God is leading them.

Now we do not always have the answers. We have mentioned this before. Do not be afraid to say, "I really do not know." There could be something that comes in the directee's prayer that you really do not understand. You simply do not have the light on it. Whatever you do, **do not guess**. This is extremely important work. It is very sacred work to walk this journey with the soul, very sacred. It is the work of a soul; it is the work of the Spirit; it is very holy. Do not guess. If you really do not know, ask the directee to take it to prayer. See what other lights you get.

We can always say, "I will take it to prayer too and the next time we meet, we can see what the Spirit is saying." Take your time; do not get ahead of the Holy Spirit. Let Him lead. If we are not careful we can end up trying to lead the Holy Spirit, not that we ever really do lead Him but we can get ahead of Him. Then you will hear, "What are you doing out there? I am not there yet!"

Learn to wait upon the Lord. We need to be sure of the Holy Spirit's actions and we need to be sure that the Holy Spirit will definitely lead the directee and that God will give him the true discernment he needs. And God will. He might not have that kind of faith at that time but the director does because God is faithful. When a person is seriously seeking the more perfect way – to be led, to be directed, to come into union – the director knows God will give that grace and He definitely will.

At times you may want to suggest a sacrifice to your directee. Sacrifices are something that we do not always think of ourselves. Oftentimes, the ones we think of ourselves are not really that sacrificial. They kind of feed us and they have to do with our own little will. So if you find that you need to offer a particular type of sacrifice to your directee at the prompting of the Spirit, do that, because if it is God's will, He will give that particular grace. It could be simple. Maybe a directee is too tired to pray in the morning; then back up and find out what time that person is going to bed at night. What is his schedule like at night? Maybe you need to impose a little sacrifice, stop all phone conversations after ten o'clock at night, or whatever. Suggest little disciplines like that to help a person to get more disciplined to pray. It will be something simple that you could suggest but it could be very sacrificial for the directee. However, remember that the directee is never forced to obey the Lord or to obey the director. All we can do is to suggest. That is all we can do. God leaves us free. We are not forced to obey God. It is always our choice.

Chapter 7

The Genuine Gift of Love

"All things work for good for those who love God..."
(Rom 8:28).

---

*"We must always pray for a genuine gift
of love for the directee – God's love."*

Some of the experts in spiritual direction tell us that if the
directee does not want freedom in the Lord, you should
terminate the direction. Isn't that interesting? If they do
not want freedom, if they do not want to take steps to
become detached and follow God's will, they are already
making a choice. Terminate the direction. They are not
ready or perhaps you are not the one to be directing them.
We might not be the right spiritual director for everybody.
We have to allow for that too. The directee must feel
comfortable with us and feel secure that we are speaking in
the name of the Lord. They have to be secure enough to be
open and to be honest. We have had retreatants who have
not been open and honest and we have had some retreat
directors here who have terminated the retreat, because

there is a lack of openness and honesty with what is expected. If you find this happening in your direction, then you can simply say, "I am not the one. You are not able to trust me enough to be open and you are not secure enough with me." Then we pray that God will lead them to someone else.

We also need to help people embrace in their prayer, the lifestyle appropriate to their state in life. That is very, very important. If they are getting things in their prayer that contradict their lifestyle or their state in life, then a spiritual director needs to reinforce the directees' state in life and bring that into the light. Our prayer cannot be divorced from our state in life. That is why we are very careful if someone, for example, is married with children and all of a sudden they feel they have a direction from the Lord to be a missionary in South America. Maybe or maybe not. Those things are always discerned. But that is normally not according to one's state in life and one's responsibilities at home. So prayer and our Christian lifestyle are inseparable. They go together and there will not be any disunity if it is the leading of the Holy Spirit. "All things," remember, "work for good for those who love God" (Rom 8:28).

We must call the directee to fulfill the duties of his state in life. It is extremely important. Otherwise, prayer can get into some mystical vagueness, totally divorced from the nitty-gritty, day to day to day. Perhaps that is why Jesus spent so much time in Nazareth – to show us the beauty of the hidden life. It is down to earth; it is practical. Authentic prayer has to go with our daily walk with the Lord. The duties of one's state in life take precedence over all the private things we would like to do.

Spiritual direction is not to be taken lightly. We must remind ourselves that it is very holy. It is a very holy, sacred ministry and there has always been that lament in the Church for hundreds of years – that there are not enough competent spiritual directors. We are seeing it today. This is why it is our hope to form you. We have not even begun to tap into the need out there. It is a good thing to go out and call people to prayer but when they respond to that call they find that they do not have anyone to direct them in the journey. There is a great need for spiritual directors.

Here are some qualities of spiritual directors above and beyond the primary quality which is humility. This comes from St. Francis de Sales. He said that directors must have three essential qualities:

1. Charity, which is love.
2. Some knowledge of theology. We need to know something of what Scripture says, what Jesus says, and what the teaching of the Church is.
3. Prudence which goes a long way in spiritual direction.

For charity, he means supernatural love. We have to see our directees as given to us directly by God Himself. We must see ourselves as kind parents who view their children as gifts directly given to them by God, to watch over, to protect and to love. We see our directees very much as spiritual children and it is important to have an unconditional love for each one – an unconditional love. Sometimes you might find that you are running out of patience, that you are running out of this kind of supernatural love. Then get back to the Lord yourself and beg Him to love that person with His love, with His heart because love is the best ingredient for spiritual direction. Love knows; it knows things. It is extremely important to constantly love a directee with no expectations, no time limit – "Lord, when are they going to learn? When are they ever going to surrender? When are they going to give this up? When are they going to see? When are they going to quit fighting?" We have to be careful there; just let the Lord lead and help that person to follow. We must always pray for a genuine gift of love for the directee, God's love.

In spiritual direction, we must learn to be very, very kind, very, very gentle – firm and open and honest – but very kind. We must be careful that the directee does not end up directing us. This can happen in very subtle ways. It can happen because when people pray and they come to us as a spiritual director, they will usually say, "Well, this is what God said! This is what the Lord said!" They are dropping the Lord's name right there. We must discern at this point; do not just assume that it is the Lord when a directee says, "The Lord said I am to do this or not to do that." All of a sudden, they are directing us because they have made their own discernment that it is the Lord. Maybe it is and maybe it is not.

> *"The main goal of spiritual direction is to bring others to spiritual perfection."*

We hear of many visionaries in our Church today. We are told that they have spiritual directors. Some of the directors are very visible theologians in the Church today. Many theologians, believe it or not, have a gift of theology but they do not have a gift of discernment. They will say, "Well, the visionary said God said this," and they accept it. So many, many people are directing their directors. We have probably all tried it. I tried it. Thanks be to God I had a strong director who picked up on it right away and called me on it – "I am directing you!" Usually, people who pray and who want a serious relationship with the Lord are strong-willed people. We want to be strong-willed, not self-willed. There is a difference. We want to be strong-willed so that we are determined, so that we make a commitment and can stand firm. But that strong will can sometimes be a detriment; it can get in our way. We can, all of sudden, try to direct the very person who is trying to direct us. So be careful that you are not allowing a directee to direct you because "The Lord said and I got this from God and this is what Jesus said." Be sure you really look at such statements very cautiously. Usually the message will be mixed. There might be some things the Lord said and some things the directee is saying. This is where good discernment comes in. As a spiritual director, you are discerning all the time.

The main goal of spiritual direction is to bring others to spiritual perfection which means that you may have to

> *"Spiritual direction is an exciting ministry."*

confront when necessary. You need to follow the Church's guidelines. You need to know something about the way the Spirit leads souls. However, you have to be careful that you do not have two blind guides here trying to lead each other. St. Francis de Sales says that we need some kind of knowledge of theology in order to avoid the situation of the blind leading the blind. He said, "We need some of the authoritative teaching of the Church." Spiritual directors need to maintain an ongoing study and review of theology. It is good to re-read at times the basic Catechism so that you will know the Church's teachings. Be sure you know what the teaching of the Church is. Right there, you have your discernment. Lots of times people write in about something. Should I do this or should I do that? We just simply write back, "This is the teaching of the Church. This is your discernment. The Church has already discerned that." There isn't anything else to discern there.

You must know something of Scripture too. Most people who pray do have some knowledge of Scripture. Many have an experiential knowledge of Scripture which comes both from discernment and when God just opens the Scripture to a person in a mystical way.

When I came home from the cloister my spiritual director saw that many people started coming to me for spiritual direction. I imposed a very strict schedule upon myself to protect my own prayer life, because they kept coming and coming. He suggested that I look for people who had a degree in spiritual direction. That way, I could refer a lot of my potential directees to them. I thought that sounded like a wonderful idea so I met with a lot of these spiritual directors. When it was over, I realized that it was not nearly so important to have a degree in spiritual direction as it was to be a person of prayer, a person attentive to the guidance of the Holy Spirit. You do not have to be ashamed or feel inferior if you do not have a degree in spiritual direction. You do need to know some theology and some of the teachings of the Church but you really need to know the Holy Spirit and how He wants to direct a particular soul.

We always want to form people into the likeness of Jesus. In the Gospels we are told that God wants us to look like Jesus, to begin talking like Jesus and acting like Jesus and loving like Jesus. It is all about Jesus. Eventually, spiritual direction has to go back to the Gospel.

A spiritual director needs to have a well-balanced understanding of the spiritual life, but we do not have to know every little thing. When you really read the lives of the saints, you will see how differently each of them was led. I'm thinking right now of Teresa of Avila and her seven mansions. The information God gave her is wonderful. She is a Doctor of the Church. But here comes another Carmelite, one of her own daughters, the Little Flower, who is as different from Teresa as night is from day. The Spirit did not lead the Little Flower at all the way He led Teresa of Avila. Then you have Elizabeth of the Trinity. She was not led like either one. Her journey is quite different from that of the Little Flower and Teresa of Avila. There is also John of the Cross, another Carmelite. His journey is totally different too. So you have to be careful that you do not put people in boxes. We must allow the Spirit to lead that soul the way He wants to lead. That is why spiritual direction is an exciting ministry. It is a beautiful ministry. You are always learning something yourself about the beauty of God and His tender love of souls and how detailed and interested He is in each particular person.

> *"God wants us to look like Jesus."*

St. Francis de Sales says that a third quality for a good director is prudence. That is good judgment. Prudence is a gift, a tremendous gift. It is a supernatural gift which comes from the Holy Spirit. You can see where the Holy Spirit is a key player. Our Lady said, "When you have the Holy Spirit, you have everything." This is part of the "everything". He knows how to direct, so let Him direct you and grant you this gift of prudence. Beg for the grace to listen to what the directee says, while at the same time being attentive to the unspoken words and actions that the

Holy Spirit will reveal to you within. That is that gift of wisdom. You are listening to both things at the same time. "I'm listening, Holy Spirit, to what this person is saying, but help me listen to what You are saying. What is it that You really want me to hear? Otherwise, I don't really know how to direct according to what You want me to see and hear." We want to see clearly what the Holy Spirit is revealing and we want to hear what the Holy Spirit wants us to say to the directee. If you do not yet have the information you need from the Spirit, wait until you do. Just let the directee continue to talk. You do not have to come back right away until you have more information from the Holy Spirit and that would usually be something incredibly simple. You will hear it. You will know it. So we have to be able, ourselves, as directors, to discern between what the Holy Spirit is saying and our own, very good ideas. Usually we have very good ideas because we are walking the walk ourselves. If we are people of prayer, we have some basic ideas. We have to be careful to discern the difference here. We have to obey the promptings of the Holy Spirit.

> *"We have to obey the promptings of the Holy Spirit."*

46

Chapter 8

A Ministry of Listening

"...listen, that you might have life" (Is 55:3).

"The result of proper direction should be that the directee needs less guidance rather than more."

Father Lieberman, a great spiritual director quoted by Thomas Green in *The Friend of the Bridegroom*, says this, "We must never attempt to inspire a soul with the personal taste of the director and individual attractions or lead the directee after our own way of acting, or our own peculiar point of view." He said, "A director that would act thus, will often turn souls from God's own guidance and oppose the action of divine grace in them." That is pretty serious, isn't it? We can actually oppose God's action in a soul. So we need to listen to determine where the soul is receiving light. Where is the soul animated? Then, we urge the soul to follow and allow the grace to flow – not to be blocked. Sometimes, if we speak too quickly, we can block the very thing for which we are listening. It did not happen because we already interrupted. When we interrupt, the Holy Spirit just stops. I learned this years ago when I had a little parakeet. I thought there was something wrong with him because he was not talking. So I went back to the bird store and said, "You know, I think maybe there is something wrong. My bird doesn't talk." I really learned a wonderful lesson. I was a new Catholic at the time. The salesman said, "Well, first of all, you are probably speaking at your own speed, in your own natural rhythm. When you teach a bird to talk you have to slow down. Secondly, you might be doing all the talking." I thought, "You've got that right!" As long as we were talking or the minute we started to talk, that parakeet would listen. They do not talk when you are talking. They listen. I asked the Lord, "There is a lesson in here, isn't there?"

"That is right. As long as you keep talking, I listen. If you want Me to talk, you start to listen."

So we must be careful that we do not do too much talking and interrupt what a directee is still saying. Wait until he develops what his thought or insight or revelation is. Try to keep on the straight and narrow. That is the beauty of John the Baptist – he was incredibly focused. We have to steer away from a lot of excess conversation. In spiritual direction, you do not want to waste a lot of time in small talk other than what might be just necessary to get the directee at ease. But then be very disciplined. You do not want to waste any time inquiring about a lot of other things in spiritual direction other than the spiritual journey of the directee himself. Stay on track. Advice given should be brief and to the point. The result of proper direction should be that the directee needs less guidance rather than more.

It is always best to give a little less than too much. When we try to offer too much direction, we can start with the Lord and then, all of a sudden, we can be outside of what the Lord would say. We can get away from simplicity very quickly and that is getting away from God. We can give a directee too much, too much, too much direction. You have to be careful. The experts say, "No amount of study can give good spiritual dis-

> *"Directors need to constantly withdraw into themselves."*

cernment" – no amount of study. We will learn some of the guidelines for good discernment but ultimately, it is gift. It comes through experience. It comes through watching the way the Lord is leading. Do I know His voice? If I do, how do I know it? How do I know His voice from other voices? How does my knowing know that? Once you know His voice in your own prayer life, you are going to know it in the directee as well. Even though He may be saying different things, it is the same voice; it is the same God. Directors need to constantly withdraw into themselves.

There can be times when you find you are just not rested enough to take a spiritual direction appointment. Be careful about that. If you try to go into spiritual direction when you are tired, you will not be able to really hear what the directee is saying – it will just bounce off of you. You will not be able to absorb it into your spirit, into your heart. So be careful that you are not overly fatigued. You want to have a heart that is rested and open to receive whatever that directee says. You have to learn to accept yourself as you are, your own limitations, your own weaknesses as well as your own strengths. You have to feel comfortable with yourself. You have to be able to see yourself as an imperfect being, still struggling in different areas as well and

49

bringing that to your own prayer. But the main thing to remember is that you want to bring your best self to this ministry. You want a heart that is open, gentle and loving.

It can be very helpful to a directee when the director can share a dimension of faith experience. If a director has had experiences of God through the faith walk, it will help the directee to share it. It is not that you are simply talking about your experience, but you know, for example, that God is faithful because you have experienced that in your own life. You can comfort that person; you can give that person encouragement, support. You have a hope; you have a faith. You have an insight into how God wants to do things. It helps you to walk the walk with the directee if you have been on the journey yourself. Simply put, a director has to have first experienced the love of God. If you have not experienced God's love yourself, how in the world can you even talk about it with somebody else? How are you going to give it to somebody else? How are you going to encourage somebody else that God loves them and to wait for the experience and to beg for the experience? So you can see that your own faith walk, even though you do not have to share those experiences, will be very useful to you in direction.

> *"God is always the answer."*

A spiritual director has to be in touch with his own sinfulness, his own brokenness, his own needs and he has to be on guard not to try to solve the problems of the directee. That is a tendency which must be avoided. We live in a culture in which we want to fix everything. Someone has a problem and we want to try to fix it. Spiritual directors have to be careful not to try to fix it but to work together

50

with the directee. "Let's ask the Lord about this together." You might even want to take some time right then to pray with your directee or to have them journal more. But let's seek God. Let's bring God into this situation because God is always the answer. He is the answer.

> *"We want to always maintain the ability to listen to the directee, and to the Holy Spirit, to nurture that wisdom gift of the two-fold listening."*

Spiritual directors can't make anything happen. When I came out of the cloister and started to give spiritual direction I had the tendency to want to fix everything. I would find all sorts of ways to fix things until my spiritual director spotted that little tendency in me. "You don't have to fix anything. You are there to pray and to take them to God and he will fix it." We have to learn to avoid the tendency to make everything right. Remember that God wants to make everything right even more than we do. I guess we just have to get out of His way. But it is our prayer that is really going to connect that person with God, so we want to work it through together.

We need to have some basic psychological information. We do not have to be psychologists. But we have to know a little bit about psychological awareness and we need to have the humility to recognize when the directee is entering into an area beyond our capabilities as a spiritual director. We have to be able to recognize when they might need the help of a professional psychologist or psychiatrist. Work together with that professional person because psychology

51

and theology can work together. They definitely work together. We have to be careful that we do not go into an area that is beyond our expertise but rather, in all humility, direct people to others for different levels of help.

Monsignor Rossage was head of all spiritual directors in the United States when I made my discernment retreat; he was a very good director. He simply says that spiritual directors need the ability to listen. It sounds simple, doesn't it? People pay psychiatrists today just to have someone to listen to them. Listening is probably a ministry that is almost extinct today. People do not listen to each other even, let alone to God. It is wonderful if we really have that ability to listen, listen to the point where we are able to take the directee's words into ourselves. You know when you are in the presence of someone who is listening to you; you know when your words are being absorbed and the other person is really receiving what you are saying. Have you ever said something to somebody and you know that they are not listening? They are just not listening. So we want to be good listeners. We always want to maintain the ability to listen to the directee and to the Holy Spirit, to nurture that wisdom gift of the two-fold listening.

We want to be able to affirm the directee in their struggles. We do not affirm people nearly enough in our culture. There is very little affirmation. I do not think you can possibly affirm someone too much. We need to affirm, affirm, affirm and encourage them in their struggles. This is another way of giving them hope. It is a way of helping the directee to know that there is always light at the end of the tunnel. We simply hope – not long term – but we encourage them just to take one day at a time.

I knew someone who had escaped from a communist country. She was telling us how they escaped. Their guide was extraordinary. The guide kept saying, "It is just another day's journey. Just a day's journey and it is all going to be changed." They were so tired; they were hungry; they were thirsty. They had to go over tremendous mountainous areas and through a lot of dangers, a lot of pitfalls. He would say, "It is going to be another day's journey." Then when they would get to another crest he would tell them, "It is just beyond there. We are so close." The psychology he was using was to give them hope. They walked miles and days and days and they made it to freedom. My friend told me, "Had he told us, 'It is umpteen miles. It is going to take us a whole week to reach the shoreline where help will be,'" she would have given up. This is what we do in direction. We say, "Just a little bit more and the growth is going to come. It is going to come." In the meantime you are begging, "God, hurry, hurry!"

Saint Claude de la Colombière was a wonderful spiritual director in his day. He said, "Distrust of self is very, very important in directing others." This is also true of one's own spiritual life. It is very necessary when directing others to distrust yourself, your own wisdom, your own knowledge. Be sure you are receiving from the Lord at all times. After we affirm the directee, we may have to help him to confront, or to challenge him in areas that need to be challenged, maybe areas of his life that actually need to be changed. This is where spiritual direction can compliment the Sacrament of Reconciliation. We can challenge. Why is this the same sin week after week or month after month? What are you doing about it? Maybe suggest something very simple that can be done and support him in that decision and, of course, intercede for that grace so he can change.

One of the beauties of spiritual direction itself is that it calls the directee to accountability. None of us does very well if we are not accountable to anybody. That's the child in us, I guess. But we need to be accountable. Spiritual direction calls one to accountability. Spiritual directors also help to clarify things for a person. A spiritual director can put things in a proper perspective. When we are so close to something, our vision can get cloudy. We cannot see up-close. A spiritual director is very objective and disin-terested. He can help put things in proper perspective.

So spiritual direction means we are entering into people's lives only for their growth in faith, their awareness of God, to help them become aware of God. We can point out so many things in their lives as we begin to know them. This is God moving here. This is God preventing this. This was God. This was God; were they not seeing that? That can help build their faith tremendously. We want to help people become aware of the presence of God, not just within, not just in their prayer life but in their entire life, so that they can live and move and have their whole being enveloped in this tremendous God who is and who was and who always will be. Amen.

Chapter 9

Disposition of the Directee

"And Mary kept all these things, reflecting on them in her heart" (Lk 2:19).

"Spiritual direction can be frightening because it will reveal things to us that we might not have seen before."

Oftentimes, a person starts to seek spiritual direction because there is a turning point in his life. Something is happening in a person's life that makes him start thinking about finding a spiritual director. Any significant change can provoke the sense of need. It could be for some a midlife crisis, or maybe a notable change in one's prayer life or life situation. Maybe somebody has entered into a new relationship with somebody that requires more insight or illumination, direction of some kind. Maybe it is a new job, a new task, a new career; new expectations might be placed upon a person. It can be any of those or others that make one think, "I think I need direction. I think I need some wisdom. I think I need some help." This is a time when a person will begin to seek a spiritual director. You will find, when we speak of spiritual directors and directees, that if you are a spiritual director it is only because you have been a directee first. It is in our time spent as a directee that we learn a lot about spiritual direction and some of its techniques.

In the beginning stages, you might find that your directee has some fear and may be afraid to follow; he may be afraid of God. He may be afraid to discover that into which God is inviting him. Perhaps he is afraid of sharing his life with someone in such a deep and intimate way. Some are even afraid of authority. There can be any number of fears in the beginning stage. The director in this situation has to be very patient and assured that in God's time, he will be of great service. The director needs to help the person accept God's invitation to begin another phase of his life, another stage of the journey. Each of our lives goes in stages, and the journey is always an invitation.

Spiritual direction can be frightening because it will reveal things to us that we might not have seen before. We may not have seen it before because we just didn't have anybody to share it with, to get it out into the light, to get somebody else's point of view on it.

So how then can we profit from spiritual direction and how can a directee profit? You will find it is pretty much one and the same. First of all, we need to realize, whether we are the director or the directee, that spiritual direction is a gift from God. It is a gift. It's a very, very beautiful gift. We really need to appreciate direction. Some of the theologians tell us that even if the director is not a saint or a dynamic director, nevertheless, that director by virtue of the ministry, is speaking in the name of Jesus and is acting as

God's instrument at that particular time. It is important for us to be comfortable with our director and to believe that he is speaking in the name of Jesus for us.

The ideal disposition of a directee would be that of Our Lady. Mary is the best example of the perfect directee. You may not have ever thought of her in that way – as a directee – but she was directed, of course, by God and she was filled with the Holy Spirit. It was during my prayer time one day, that Our Lady let me understand that her director was the Holy Spirit. She said that He taught her everything she ever knew about love. At that time I hadn't really realized that she herself was a directee, that she was being directed. She had the best disposition as a directee because she understood what God wanted to do for her. She understood that God wanted the best for her even though right at that moment it might not have seemed that way. She took a big risk in what God was asking of her. She knew that it would only be to proclaim His greatness. She gave God her "yes" even though she didn't perfectly understand everything at the time, and she pondered these things in her heart. Directees ponder. We may not always understand some of the things that the spiritual director might throw at us or with which he might challenge us. It may be some new thought or a new concept.

So we ponder. Our Lady had the perfect attitude because she always did whatever – whatever – God said. The directee who does that gives great joy to the heart of a director. If we have a spiritual director in our own life, our attitude should be that we are going to do whatever the Lord is indicating to us. Our Lady's life speaks of the basis of spiritual direction. She was constantly discerning, which is what we need to do. This is why a director is important in our life. Once the discernment process is over, just do it! That is the ideal disposition of a directee.

> *"Both the director and the directee need a strong desire to grow in the awareness of God."*

Openness and the desire to grow and to profit from direction is extremely important. If you are going to be committed to it then you must be truly committed. As a directee, you must make that commitment. A spiritual director needs to make that commitment too. This is such holy work. It is like being on holy ground because only God knows the deep, intimate being of a soul. Spiritual direction is very, very holy work.

Both the directee and the director need a strong desire to grow in the awareness of God and in the response to the living God. That takes commitment; effort must be put into the relationship. We do not take it casually. A directee needs to respect the director as the authority in the spiritual walk – sharing the way, pointing the way, becoming sign posts along the way. We must have great respect for our directors. Criticism needs to be avoided. If you find that you are starting to become critical of your director, take that to prayer and see what the Lord is saying because it will really hinder your walk if you start to become critical of your director in any way.

Is spiritual direction itself confidential? Yes it is; it is very confidential. In other words you can certainly trust your spiritual director. Trust is one of the main principles of spiritual direction. Trust, of course, has to be nurtured. It has to grow. It takes time to get acquainted, to become comfortable with your director. It takes time to build that trust. You may not want to throw everything out to your director all at once. You might want to see how he is going to respond. Directors should be very aware of this and do everything they can to make the directee feel as comfortable and at home in their presence as possible.

A director must understand the struggles and the trials of the directee as much as possible. Compassion goes a long way. Directors are not there to judge. Directors are there to share and to help carry the load and to point the way to freedom. It must always lead to God, always to God. Absolute honesty is necessary if you want to progress rapidly. Honesty is very, very important. As a directee, withholding information from your director (perhaps, to appear holier or for all different sorts of reasons) can impede the progress. We cannot deceive God, but lots of times, out of fear, we may think to ourselves, "Well, if my spiritual director knew everything about me, he might reject me. He might not love me." You may have experienced that in your life. There are fears to overcome on the directee's part and so it is very important for the director to affirm, affirm, affirm and have that gentleness and that compassion so that the directee will become more at ease and will be more open and very honest.

The better the director knows the directee, the better the director will be able to guide. You need information. You need those lights. You need those insights. A director also needs this honesty in order to direct. So if you are a directee and you are having difficulty speaking about certain things, come right out and tell that to the director. Let the director know right away there are certain things that may be uncomfortable or difficult for you to share. Let the director know so he can begin asking certain questions to help put you at ease. If you are a director, that's what you need to do as well. As a directee, when you relate this to your director, try to be brief and bottom line so that the director can get it very clearly.

Docility is especially important if you are a directee. That means being open and willing to carry out the advice, the counsel, of the director. If you ever feel that the director is saying something that you believe is not of God, feel free to question. If you do not understand something, or maybe feel that the director does not understand you, feel free to dialogue. A childlike attitude is always important. The directee needs to be accepted and encouraged in his own beautiful uniqueness.

Chapter 10

Spiritual Direction – God's Plan

"But seek first the kingdom of God (Mt 6:33).

> *"Always remember, spiritual direction is the work of God."*

St. Ignatius said that one can make no greater mistake or do greater harm than to direct others as he directs himself. That is really important. Teresa of Avila talked about that too. We cannot direct people the same way God directed us or from our own experiences. Our own experiences may be shared at times and may be helpful. They may be experiences that will be supportive to let somebody know, "I've been there. I know what kind of fear that is. I know what rejection is or that kind of anger," or whatever. But we have to be careful that we do not direct someone exactly the way that we have been directed ourselves. We must remember that this is the work of the Holy Spirit and the Spirit of God is going to direct each person differently. In my experience of spiritual direction, I have never, ever seen the Holy Spirit direct two people the same way – never. All the experiences are different. All their insights and descriptions are just a little bit different. They have different dreams. They have different life patterns; they have different personalities. The Spirit works with the whole person, which is why it is so beautiful. It is beautiful to watch the uniqueness of the Holy Spirit work. All we have to do is be sure we stay out of His way and pick Him up if we can, to support and affirm and encourage the directee.

Now the responsibility of the directee again is being open and looking very truthfully at oneself. In other words we have to be open to self-contemplation. Sometimes we want to look at everybody else rather than at ourselves. Peter did that. He asked Jesus, "What about John?" and Jesus said, "That is no concern of yours, Peter" (Jn 21:21-22). Don't be looking at John; do not be worried about the way other people are being directed or led or about the details of their missions or ministries or their lives. Spiritual direction requires self-confrontation, and this is very, very important. The directees – and that is all of us – have to look deep inside of themselves to find the answers. That is where the answers lie. Do no look for the answers from others.

> "God makes all things beautiful in His time."

The director is there to help guide and support the directee in the discernment process. But is it very important that the directee discover that his own mind is illumined, that he hears and knows, that he gets the truth, the insight. That might take time. It might take quite some time. That is where the intercession behind the scenes is extremely important because you cannot get ahead of God. Even though sometimes you would just like to tell the person what the answers are, God is waiting. There may be other things that God is doing until the directee arrives at that moment of truth. Those of us who have been there know that we each need to have that moment of truth, but it has to be our moment. God is gentle; God is patient. Spiritual directors have to be patient. We all have to be patient with ourselves too. God is not finished with any of us yet, thanks be to God.

We need the desire to find God's will. In spiritual direction, God wants us to bring all of our experiences to Him in the presence of the director. That means bringing the joyful experiences and the painful experiences so that all can be touched by God, all can be transformed.

> "The spiritual journey itself is a process."

This takes up our entire life, our everyday life. Spiritual direction takes in everything because God is present in everything. A spiritual director can help a person see this. "Do you see God moving there?" or "Do you see that you are here because God prevented this?" We can point a lot of things out that they might not be able to see. None of us can see ourselves up too close. Sometimes a person may think, "God is not with me; He never does anything for me!" or, "Where were You, God, when this happened?" Oftentimes the spiritual director can say, "Oh but look at this! Look at this point of view." You can share a different angle. Anyone who is under spiritual direction knows what I am talking about because you have been there and you know how that moment of truth is important, but it has to be your moment of truth. God makes all things beautiful in His time. We must remember that these things all happen in God's time. We must be patient, both the director and the directee, and not be in a hurry. God will always come through right on time – in His time.

The spiritual journey itself is a process and it takes time. It takes time to be set free from attachments. It takes time to grow. It took time for us to get attached to certain things, certain habits, or maybe even to certain sins. So we have to allow that time. But with God's grace and through Our Lady's intercession the process is hurried up quite a bit, particularly when we are wholly committed to it. The directee needs to be very open with the director and this means that the directee needs courage, humility and a certain amount of maturity. He must acknowledge, "I need direction. I need help and I am willing to accept what the director is saying because I know that that director is doing this in love." In this relationship it is important that the directee is able to trust the director and know that this person has his best interest at heart.

Now there might be (and this is not too terribly uncommon) a need to change spiritual directors. St. John of the Cross says that a director must always lead us back to the humility of Christ. So be careful there. Ask yourself, "Is this director doing this?" While the Church herself safeguards the right and freedom of individuals to switch to other directors and confessors, the saints and the theologians tell us to be sure to have valid reasons. For example, if you, yourself, are not being open, if you do not put your confidence in your director, that might not be a valid reason. You may have a deeper problem with yourself. However, if you cannot maintain respect for your director, if you don't have any confidence, without this respect and this openness, little will be accomplished. You are just not going to open; none of us is going to open up to someone if we do not have confidence in that person. Also you might switch for other reasons. You might validly feel that the director's views are just too natural rather than supernatural. You might feel this is not a person of prayer or that he is speaking out of his natural spirit. You might feel that his opinions are much too strong. There are people who are very opinionated. If you feel that, you are not going to have the openness and trust you will need. So, once again, the direction will not go very far. You might feel that your spiritual director lacks knowledge, spiritual knowledge, knowledge of God, knowledge of the ways of the Spirit. You might find that your spiritual director lacks prudence or discretion. These, saints and theologians tell us, can be very valid reasons for beginning to seek another spiritual director.

Now there are some false reasons though, so I want to point those out too. You know how we are – we have our own rationale; we can rationalize anything. We might want to change spiritual directors because we are bored. By that I mean, we are tired of listening to the same advice, probably because we have not done it, so we hear our spiritual director go over and over the same thing. That might be simply because we are choosing not to respond to that direction so we are bored. We are tired of hearing that. We can go to any director and boredom can set in if we do not respond.

Some people, believe it or not, change spiritual directors for reasons of vanity. They hear that a certain director is well known or is supposed to be a top spiritual director somewhere, and for that reason they want to say, "Well, so and so is my spiritual director." Be careful not to seek a spiritual director for those reasons.

Some people want another director because they are restless. They feel that they should be arriving at perfection much more quickly. We want everything **now**, so we say, "This is not the person for me because he is not getting me into this perfection right away. I still have my faults. I still have my hang-ups. I still have my sins. I am not getting anywhere." Restlessness sets in.

It may be that there are things that you really want to hide, some shame or a weakness within yourself, and you do not want to confront these things so you go to another director. There are some people who want more than one director. Some of the priests that I used to know quite well when I was a new convert, used to call these people "sacristy saints." I asked, "What do you mean by that?" They said, "Well, they go from priest to priest to priest and they'll tell this priest one thing and they think that they will get some direction from God. Then, they will go to another priest for something else. So there are about five different directors in their life and there isn't one person that knows them totally." That is the rationale behind this behavior.

In reality, it is a false humility and it is running isn't it? So they can say, "Well, Father said this," or, "my spiritual director said that," but maybe they forget to tell you that they have four spiritual directors telling them other things also. We do not direct people here if they have other spiritual directors. It is not a good idea. Let the person have whomever they want and move on, because there could be a conflict there. There is division. You are not going to get to know the whole person and the whole movement of God within that person and that is a disservice to the other person who is trying to direct at the same time. St. Claude de la Colombière said, "Choose one person to whom you will reveal your life or to whom you will give your interior life." He said, "To change one's director every year [and some people do] is equivalent to never making any progress." The saints are very strict on this. They take it very, very seriously.

66

How do we find a spiritual director? How do we help other people find a spiritual director? Begin by asking the Lord. God knows who is the best one for us at a particular stage of our journey and where that person is. It could be that there is a spiritual director for one stage of the journey but that person may not have

"The spiritual director must be under spiritual direction himself."

the experience needed to take us where God wants us to be for the next stage of the journey. I have seen directees bypass their spiritual directors. It can happen. So, if that happens to you, ask God to show you another director. Keep in mind that He does want it. It takes faith to believe that He will supply that person.

Even though we are living in a Church with a tremendous shortage of spiritual directors, God will supply because He wants us to grow in relationship with Him even more than we desire it. He knows we grow so much more quickly if we have a director, and He will send a competent guide. You might just hear a name. You might just get somebody in prayer. You might bump into this person. You never know. But, if you ask, God will be faithful and provide. It might be someone that you do not even expect or ever thought maybe would be a director, but you will know. Again, test the waters and if you find that you are just not comfortable then, of course, be open with that spiritual director and ask God to show you someone else.

There will be differences in personality, and spiritual directors must be open enough to enter into the uniqueness of the other person. You may find that your directee is a person with whom you would not normally share things about yourself. Yet, this is the person God has sent to you. This is the person who is believing and trusting in you to be an instrument of God. You have to be open enough to enter into that person's life and their own personal experiences.

The spiritual director must be under spiritual direction too. That is extremely important. It is a beautiful canopy, isn't it? It is a beautiful covering. If you are going to direct someone then you also need to be directed yourself. Always remember, spiritual direction is the work of God.

Chapter 11

Tough Love

"Let the word of Christ dwell in you richly, as in all wisdom you teach and admonish one another" (Col 3:16).

"Spiritual directors challenge,
they correct, but
they never, never condemn."

There are times in spiritual direction when correction is needed. Jesus is the perfect spiritual director and Jesus did not mince words. He knew how to correct and when something or somebody needed to be corrected, He did it. He did not condemn them for their actions or for their lack of action but He did correct and challenge them in their faith. Spiritual directors do that. They challenge, they can correct, but they never, never condemn.

Jesus did not reason with people when He saw they needed to be corrected. Parents know that doesn't go too far. If you need to correct, you need to correct. But there is a beautiful, gentle way of doing it. The goal of all correction is to bring about a healing process. It is healing the one we love. It is healing the one we are directing. It is preventing a brother or sister from hurting themselves or others, so look at it that way.

The correction is a beautiful healing process. Always correct gently, with patience and not in any hurting way. Make sure that you go into prayer before you correct a directee. God will go first and prepare the way. Ask Him to prepare that heart to receive it. It makes all the difference in the world if that person is ready to receive. When you do correct, do so privately. Scripture says if a person is just not going to listen and it is something that is doing damage outside of spiritual direction, something that is doing damage to the community, then you might have to bring it to the attention of someone in authority in the community. That does happen sometimes. Sometimes when an infraction is brought to the person privately and they don't want to do anything about it, then you will have to go beyond just the directee. As Jesus said, "then take it to the elders." Take it to the community; take it to those in authority.

> *"The biggest hindrance to good spiritual direction is failing to be open and honest."*

You always correct with wisdom. Theologians and saints tell us that wisdom comes from God. In Colossians 3:16 Paul says, "Let the word of Christ dwell in you richly, as in all wisdom you teach and admonish one another." Correction, done in this light, is healing and brings the wisdom of God to others.

70

The directee's deep desire for God and the relationship of the spiritual director will give both of them strength, support and courage. It will help the director confront and it will help the directee to receive because of the relationship that is established. When there is love you can do a lot of things. The fruit of correction is that it brings wisdom, it brings comfort and it will always bring peace, because it will always bring God's perfect will.

> *"We must get rid of the need to protect or defend ourselves."*

The biggest hindrance to good spiritual direction is failing to be open and honest, hiding our deepest self from the director. The director needs to know all of us – as much as we can share, the whole person. A hindrance would be that need to protect or defend ourselves. Thomas Merton calls this the greatest obstacle to grace in our relationship with the director, this need to protect ourselves. We might want to protect ourselves from everybody else out there but not from our director. This is the one person that we can trust and with whom we can be open in the deep, deep things of the soul, of the heart. We must get rid of the need to protect or defend self. In other words, we must get rid of self-justification.

The relationship between the director and the directee is friendly and sincere. It has to be personal. We have to know the person and we let that person get to know us in many ways as well.

We have to be willing to go into the desert with Jesus and the Holy Spirit to confront the deep things within ourselves – both as a director and as a directee. We have to confront sin. We have to do that. It is here, in spiritual direction – the desert – where we can confront. This is where Jesus confronted Satan and the temptations. All these different temptations have to be confronted here, in spiritual direction. Perhaps one of the reasons that we go to confession over and over and over saying the same thing, is because we have not yet gone deep enough into the desert to

> *"We are called to be winners."*

confront the very root, the very source, of where the temptation is and where it begins. We really have to go into the deep part of the desert to have this victory over sin and Satan's kingdom. As we confront these things within ourselves more and more, we will be able then to help others go into this part of the desert without fear because this is a deep part of solitude. This battle takes place in the silence and solitude. This is where God dwells and this is where the Spirit is leading us in this beautiful relationship of director and directee. Into this desert we will have the victory and we will start going through transforming union; we will start to cast aside all that is hindering us. This is where we run the race, and we want to win. We are called to be winners.

Appendices

The following section contains various meditations that Mother Nadine has used throughout the years at retreats, conferences and in her writings. These meditations cover many spiritual issues but generally focus on varying aspects of inner healing through a prayerful encounter with Jesus.

While anyone can benefit from these exercises, they might be of particular help to spiritual directors whose directees are experiencing blocks along their spiritual journeys.

These meditations are designed to be prayed, not read. When using one of these spiritual exercises, observing the following guidelines will enhance one's spiritual sensitivity and help prepare the participant to experience Christ in a real and powerful way:

- Approach these meditations with a prayerful and contemplative disposition.
- Take your time and allow God to speak to you.
- Find a quiet place that will be devoid of distractions.
- Be patient and allow the Lord to move at His own pace and in His own way.
- Be open to each part of the meditation even if at first it might seem strange or uncomfortable.

Each meditation has been titled to give the reader a sense of its theme. In this way, each person or spiritual director can choose the exercise that best speaks to where they are at a particular time or place on their spiritual journey.

The Road to Emmaus

Close your eyes and imagine that you are walking down the road to Emmaus. It was probably a very dusty road, and it probably had a lot of stones. You might see if you can even feel what it's like to walk on those stones. See if you can experience the dust. It might be a day that was very warm; it might be noontime, with the sun beating down. The beauty of noontime is that you are right under the glory spout, in full light. St. Ignatius encourages us to try to get into the Gospel scene, get into the word, into that Scripture passage.

Each of us is there on that road, alone with Him. Share with Him now your strongest feelings or whatever is most in your mind. It might be a fear you have or anger. It might be a desire to change. It might be something for which you are very grateful or something for which you are not grateful, a problem. If you do not know what to share, just feel the tension in your body and see what your body is saying. You can talk to Him about that. When you finish, just look into His eyes and take in what He is saying to you from the Scriptures. Jesus will use His own words, where He is or where He has been or maybe what another person in Scripture is feeling or when He has felt the same way you do. Just bask in His response until your heart also can burn with the love that is in His heart.

Spend a few minutes just taking in what He says to you. Maybe He will help you identify another Gospel scene, a word, a Scripture of which you might say, "That is exactly what is going on in my life right now!" Feel free to use your imagination in whatever way is most comfortable for you. But remember that you do not have to use your imagination. It might be that you will experience something

Jesus is saying or a Scripture He is going to bring to your mind, maybe just a touch of His presence. The main thing is simply to write down what is in your heart and write down Jesus' response to you.

Forgiving My Family

We are going to go through an exercise now for the healings of memories. When you feel that the Lord is leading you to a particular memory, just stay there and allow the Lord to take you through it.

Lord, we are very grateful. We are grateful that there is no time in Your world. We are grateful that You can walk back throughout all our lives – all the way back to the very moment we were conceived – and You can heal us even then. We are grateful that You can free us from all those things that may have caused us difficulties at the moment of our conception, whether we were conceived in an act of love or whether we were an accident. As we were being formed in our mother's womb, You were there to heal. You were there to touch. I ask You, Jesus, to enter into my heart and touch now those life experiences that need to be healed. Bring Your love to every part of my heart. Lord, wherever You discover the wounded child, touch that child; console that child and release that child. Walk back through my life, Lord, to the very moment when I was conceived and cleanse my bloodlines; free me from those things that may have exerted a negative influence at that moment. Lord, bless me as I was being formed within my mother's womb and remove all barriers to wholeness that may have affected me during those months of confinement.

Grant me a deep desire to want to be born and heal any physical or emotional trauma that could have harmed me during the birth process. Thank You, Lord, for being there to receive me into Your arms at the very moment of my birth to welcome me into existence and assure me that You would never fail me or desert me. Jesus, I ask You to surround my infancy with Your light and touch those memories that keep me from being free.

Lord, if I needed more of a mother's love, send me Your mother, Mary, to provide whatever is lacking. Ask her to hold me close, to rock me, to tell me stories and to fill in those empty parts of me that need the comfort and love only a mother can give. Lord, maybe for some reason my mother herself was not in an atmosphere of love. Perhaps her environment was the result of poverty or discord. Maybe she was overworked or tired or fearful. Maybe there were problems in the marriage. Maybe she was not being loved. Whatever the reason, our spirits picked this up long before we were ever delivered. We ask You, Lord, to replace for us what may have been lacking within us and remove from our spirits any anger, resentment or whatever has been there that is not of You. For many of us, our mothers were in labor for hours and maybe this has had a tremendous effect upon us as an infant. Perhaps someone here was a blue baby, a breech baby or born by instrument. We pray, Lord, that You would heal us of the birth pains, the trauma, whatever it was we went through in being born. Remove any doubt, any fear, and any feeling of insecurity we may have incurred in passing from our mother's womb.

Rid us, Lord, of any guilt with which we may be burdened in having caused another suffering because of our coming into this world, especially if we perceived that we were neither wanted nor loved. We ask You, Jesus, to dispel any disappointment we may have been to our parents because they so much wanted a baby boy and we were born a little girl, or because they expected a daughter and the doctor announced, "You have a son." We pray, Jesus, that any disappointment, any frustration we may be carrying within our spirits because of having been born the wrong sex would be healed now and that from this day on, we would be allowed to become the men and women You have destined us to be. We pray, Lord, that whatever pain our coming into the world may have caused another, especially our mothers, You would heal right now with Your Precious Blood. We ask, Lord, for healing upon each one of us for that particular time in our lives.

We thank You, Jesus, for being there as we were born, to receive us anew. We just couldn't remember, Lord. Perhaps the child inside of us feels deprived in the areas of a father's love. Lord, let me be free to cry, "Abba! Daddy," with every part of my being. If I needed more of a father's love and security to assure me that I was wanted and loved very deeply, I ask You to hold me and let me feel Your strong protective arms. Give me renewed confidence and courage to face the trials of the world because I know my heavenly Father's love will support me if I stumble and fall.

Walk through my life, Lord, when others were not kind. Heal the wounds of encounters that left me frightened, that caused me to retreat into myself and erect barriers to people. Grant me, through Your healing love, a new sense of worth as a person.

Lord, we know that in the very early time of our life, we receive our identity very much from our fathers. Perhaps, Lord, we never knew our fathers because they were away or perhaps they just never came home. Perhaps we were separated from our fathers through divorce or death. Whatever the reason for the void, we ask You, Jesus, to fill in that part of our lives now with the strong tender love that can come only from a father. When we needed to have those strong arms around us and a daddy to love us, when we needed a father's advice, when we needed to feel his strength and the security of his love and he wasn't there, oh Lord, we wish that we could have experienced all of this.

But we know, Lord, that we can experience it now with our Abba. Let us know that we have never been abandoned. Let us know with certainty that there are strong arms to lean on, that we have someone watching over us and caring for us, even when we are not fully aware of it. Jesus, as a father often stoops to raise his child to his cheeks, we ask that You would now take us into Your embrace and that the warmth, the strength, the tenderness of this embrace would heal us.

Lord, we also ask for healings for all of us as we were growing up. Some of us were born into very large families and there wasn't much time for us as individuals. Now we can understand this; we can even accept it; yet there is a part of us that did not feel loved and that did not understand it as a child. So we pray today, Jesus, that You would let us know that each of us is a very favorite child; that each one of us is very important, a very special person in Your family; that each of us is unique and a very distinct individual; and that You love each one of us in a very tender and special way.

We pray, Jesus, that You would heal any hurts that may have come to us because of relationships within the family – the brother, the sister who did not accept us, who did not understand us, who did not show us the love or the kindness that we really needed to receive from him or her. Heal that part of us that never felt loved because of not receiving this love from one of our brothers or sisters.

Lord, we ask too, for healing for all of us as we went off to school. Perhaps the first real trauma in our lives came when we actually left for school the very first time. Perhaps we had never before been separated from our mothers or from our homes and the experience seemed unbearable. Some of us, Lord, were very sensitive and shy. For some of us, it was extremely difficult to be with that unknown teacher, with those unfamiliar children and in that cold classroom. Maybe, Lord, there were things that were expected of us and things that were done to us by teachers who were unkind or by classmates who did not understand us and accept us. Maybe our parents thought our C's should be B's and our B's should be A's, so we grew up thinking we could not possibly ever be good enough for anything. Jesus, we ask You to heal each of us through any of those years we spent in the classroom, particularly as some of us began to withdraw or began to fear speaking out in groups because we had been ridiculed or criticized in classroom situations. We ask, Lord, that the door within the hearts of each of us may be opened and that our tongues would be loosened and that we could allow ourselves to relate to one another in a more open and free way.

Lord, we want to ask, too, for the healings we need for our adolescent years, when we began to experience sexual maturity and it frightened us or maybe embarrassed us or caused us pain. We ask a healing on those years we spent as teenagers. We ask You to heal any doubts we had then, any fears and especially our insecurities. We ask the healing for those times when we may have been hurt in interpersonal relationships and when we were put down by others or taken advantage of or laughed at. Lord, in all of those incidents that have caused us suffering or embarrassment we ask now that You enter in. Enter into our hearts, into our deep memory, and transform all those experiences so that we remember them not with shame but with thanksgiving. Help us to appreciate the difficulties, Lord, that we, as young people, faced while growing up, while seeking our identity. Help us, Lord, to become totally whole.

Lord, as we emerge from that period of our lives and we

begin to enter into the vocation to which You called us, we ask a healing on the difficulties that came upon us. Heal us for the times when we might have failed to become professional in areas where we wanted most to succeed, for the dreams and expectations that we had but were never realized. Lord Jesus, we hold up to You now all of those unachieved longings. Some of us have been called to be wives and mothers, husbands and fathers. Some of us have been called to the religious life or to be single laypersons. Others have been called to priesthood. In whatever way You have asked us to follow You, Lord, there have been sufferings and there has been pain. We know there is no career or vocation on earth that does not entail some difficulty, some adjustment or some problem deep inside of us that needs to be healed now. So, Jesus, we pray that You would heal us in the state in life in which we find ourselves today and all that it has meant to the world around us.

Lord, we pray that with each other, we would not fear to break the bread of ourselves, that with each other we would not fear to share our cup of weaknesses – a sharing of light built not on a false ideal but on real hope with faith in ourselves and with trust in each other. We ask You, Jesus, that the life we share might truly be Your life.

Jesus, as Your love flows over us and as we find within our own hearts those things that need to be healed or to be set free, we want to praise and thank You because we know, we truly know and truly believe that the healing is being done.

Lord, we thank You especially for the words spoken to us through the prophet Isaiah: "Remember not the events of the past. The things of long ago, consider not. See, I am doing something new! Now it springs forth! Do you not perceive it" (Is 43:18-19)?

Take time with the Lord to journal whatever He brings to your mind.

The Washing of the Feet

I would like to take you through a little exercise, so get
settled. Afterwards, spend some time journaling whatever
God brings to your mind. The passage I have selected is the
Gospel scene when Jesus knelt at the feet of Peter washing
his feet. Peter did not really know how to receive that.
Jesus said, "I am among you as the one who serves. Let me
minister to you, Peter." So we are going to allow Jesus to
come to us and kneel before us. Now, that might seem a
little strange to some of you because we are taught to kneel
to Jesus, aren't we? We genuflect when we come into His
presence; we kneel. But now Jesus is saying, "I am among
you as the one who serves, so let Me minister to you."

We are actually in His presence. The room is filled with the
Holy Spirit. Just try to relax and breathe in the Holy Spirit.
When you breathe out, just breathe out the Holy Spirit, the
perfect love of the Spirit. In your imagination (if you
cannot see it in your imaginative heart, then just think it
with your thoughts) allow Jesus to come to you right where
you are, right where you are sitting. He comes and kneels
down right before you. Just relax and allow Jesus, in His
love for you, to kneel there before you. Jesus is there
kneeling at your feet. Let Him say those words to you, "I
have come to serve you. I want to serve you because then,
in turn, I am going to send you out to serve others. Let Me
kneel before you and let Me give you all that you need."

As He kneels there before you, He looks into your eyes and
you look into His eyes. As He looks into your eyes, He
sees deep, deep, inside of you. He sees every moment of
your life that you have ever lived. He sees all the heartache
you have ever had; He sees all the joy. He sees back over
the years. He sees all the times that you have been happy,

that you have been loving and generous; and He also sees those times when you have been despondent, when you felt like a failure. He sees all the blessings that you have had and He sees all the tears that you have shed. As He looks deeper and deeper He sees all of the loving things you have done, all the things that no one knows about except you – beautiful things in your life that you have always kept hidden.

He knows that you really are a beautiful person within. But He sees those blocks; He sees those negative aspects of your life that keep you from knowing what a beautiful person you really are. He sees the things that keep you from knowing that you are a loving person. Know that as He looks into your eyes, He loves you so much that He cannot stand for these blocks to be there.

As He begins to pour His love into you, He is going to be just like a magnet. His love is so pure, is so radiant, that the light that begins to come forth from Him starts to draw from you all the darkness that is within you. As He sees that darkness within you, there are little specks of guilt, little specks of rejection; there are little dark spots of unforgiveness and broken relationships. He sees those dark specks of inferiority. He knows when you have been put down, criticized, judged, and condemned.

As He kneels there before you, all of a sudden that darkness begins to be drawn from you and maybe in your mind's eye you can even sense that there is a stream of darkness pouring out from you through your heart. As it begins to come out into the light of Jesus, it is consumed by His light. Remember the Scripture that says, "Perfect love drives out fear" (1 Jn 4:18). It means that this perfect love diminishes fear and consumes it. His perfect love consumes all guilt. Perfect love consumes all feelings of rejection, all self-hate and all hostility. As He continues to kneel there, all of the little shadows of darkness begin to come out until it is no longer black streams that come forth but lighter shades of gray. All the guilt begins to break loose. All the unforgiveness breaks loose; all the unloving action begins to break loose and all of it flows from you, from the center of your being, that deep heart level, that deep unconscious level; it flows out from you, consumed in His perfect love.

Now, you begin to feel lighter, emptier, freer – no darkness, no pain, no guilt, no hurt. Jesus says to you, "This is why I came – to set you free. I came to make you a free person, that you can have joy overflowing, love overflowing all the time." As He draws this out and you become empty, His love begins to move into you. That light from Jesus begins to fill every part of your being. There is that rushing of His love, that rushing of His light going into every empty place, into every void within your life, for long has He waited for your coming home to Him. He is filling you. He is filling you. He is filling you to overflowing; every cell in your whole being is becoming immersed in His love, every thought, not only in your conscious mind, but in your deep mind. Every unconscious thought is being consumed and filled with perfect love. Jesus is making you whole. He is healing you now in every way and He says to you, "Now that you have given yourself to Me, now that you have surrendered your life to Me, I want to be in you and I want you to be in Me as I am in the Father and the Father is in Me. I want to be flesh of your flesh, bone of your bone, one with you from now throughout all of eternity, forever and ever."

As He finishes and we are being filled with His love, we give thanks to Him:

We thank You, Jesus, that You have brought each of us to

this place of total surrender and that nothing, nothing can ever separate us from this love that we are experiencing in this moment. Nothing in heaven, nothing on earth, nothing in the past, nothing in the future can ever separate us from this love that we have from the Father through You, Jesus. To You, Jesus, the Lord and savior of our life, we give You all the glory. Amen.

Healing Love

We will take a few moments here to call the Holy Spirit forth into these subconscious areas of our lives, so move into that attitude of, "I want to receive His abundant love. I want to receive all that He has for me – everything." As the Little Flower used to say, "I want everything."

As you relax, breathe in the Holy Spirit and think of the Holy Spirit completely immersing you in His love. Think of the light of Jesus moving through your being, lighting every single area of darkness within you. Try to imagine that you are kneeling now before Jesus or sitting right next to Him. Imagine that you are confessing to Him any area in your life that comes to your mind, any area of disobedience, any area where you have been unloving, any area of broken relationships.

Then, just tell Jesus, "Lord, I know that You see the darkness that is within my life and I praise You and give You thanks that Your light removes all darkness within me. I praise and thank You that I can confess to You, Jesus, that there are things unknown in my life that need to be healed.

"I offer myself as a living sacrifice, that Your healing love may remove this darkness, these negative attitudes, that You may become perfect forgiveness within my life. Jesus, I give You permission to bring to my memory any unconfessed sin in my life that I might make it right, not only before You, Lord, but also before my brothers and sisters if I have offended them in any way.

"I rejoice, Jesus, to know that You are my healer and no matter how far I have strayed from You and no matter how far I have strayed from the obedience to Your word, You love me and You forgive me with unconditional love. Jesus, as I confess my humanity to You, I receive Your love and Your forgiveness through Your blood that was shed on the cross for me.

"Jesus, as You touch us, we ask that You continue filling us with Your healing love. We know the blocks and the barriers that separate us from this love come because of those ties and those knots, those areas of bondage within, those ideas of self-condemnation that prevent us from knowing how much You really love us. So right now, we ask You to touch our mind, the mind that we think with, the mind that we listen with. If we have any conscious block about Your ability to heal, we ask that this block be removed. Jesus, if we have any doubt as to whether You love us or not, we ask that right now, You consume every doubt, that we may have perfect faith.

"Lord, in this act of obedience, we affirm that You love us and that You desire us to be whole. We know that You desire us to love the Father, that You desire for us to love one another and, Jesus, we know that it is Your greatest desire that we love ourselves. We ask that in Your love for us, in order to help each one of us to love and accept ourselves, that You touch the hurt within each one of us, that You touch the pain, the disappointment we may not even be aware of. Jesus, we ask that Your love would flow through our deep mind and touch every conflict, every anxiety. Move into every moment where there has been depression and move into every relationship where there has been any imperfection. Jesus, we ask that You move back into that deep mind and heal anything that may have been damaged by our disobedience. Lord Jesus, we ask that You remove the guilt of every sexual experience each one of us may have had, the guilt of all of the desires we have had within our mind that were never fulfilled. Remove the guilt that we have had toward ourselves for our unforgiveness and remove all the guilt of all the barriers we have allowed to build up between ourselves and any other human being.

"Thank You, Jesus, that Your healing love is moving into each one of these areas. And, Jesus, because we do not know when that sense of unworthiness came to us, we do not understand why we have been unable to accept ourselves. So we ask You, Jesus, that we may move back even further into those early years of our life. Lord, we know that our lack of self-acceptance goes back to that little child within us, whom we have so much trouble loving and accepting and really understanding.

"Jesus, we ask that as You heal us as adults, You also heal every part of the little child within us. So we bring the little child that we are to You and we ask forgiveness for all the times we blamed that little child for the many things he or she had done. That little child was hurt so many times and no one ever knew it. Jesus, take that little child within us into Your arms and whisper deep into the ear, 'I love you!' We ask for a miracle of the Holy Spirit that Your words can penetrate beyond the ear into that deep unconsciousness, so that the little child may truly know Your unconditional love.

"Jesus, we ask now that the little child within us and the adult that we are may be integrated, that we may get to know each other, that we may get to understand each other, that we may have that communication of perfect love with no judgmental attitudes, no blame, no condemnation. We thank You, Jesus, for bridging the gap between the adult we are and the little child that is hurting still within. We thank You that You are the healer and that right now You are bringing us into total integration and total wholeness.

"We accept that stillness, that inner stillness of Your peace. We affirm our confidence in Your love for us, knowing that You will continue transforming each one of us until we have become integrated as one person within and restored to complete wholeness, that we may be an expression of perfect love. We beg Your love for that beautiful grace of perfect reconciliation, not only to our fellow man, not only to the Father, but that expression and reconciliation of perfect love to ourselves. We pray this especially through Mary's Immaculate Heart, through Our Lady, Queen of Peace, and in Jesus' name. Amen."

Daily Reconciliation

In order to reach maximum effectiveness, set aside approximately ten minutes for this exercise. Find a quiet place where you will not be interrupted. Begin by picturing yourself as a little child sitting with Jesus and holding His hand.

After pondering this scene for a moment, begin to walk forward through the years, still holding Jesus' hand. As you walk through time, ask the Holy Spirit to bring to your mind every unhealed or painful relationship you have ever experienced. When you come to a situation where you have been unable to forgive someone, simply picture that person's face before you or recall them mentally, and ask Jesus to bless them with His grace and forgiveness.

When you come to a relationship for which you have never asked forgiveness ask Jesus to touch you with His grace and forgiving love to heal any guilt you may have.

Repeat this exercise each day. Although the feeling of an adequate sense of forgiving or being forgiven may take time, repeatedly bringing Jesus to those unforgiven moments can eventually bring the needed reconciliation.

Forgiving My Mother and My Father

Get comfortable. Relax and let go of all tension. Imagine now that Jesus is right where you are and place your head upon His shoulder. You might consider allowing Him to put His arm around you. Know that He is your friend. As you sit with Him let your thoughts become very secure. Ask to receive the experience of a sense of perfect peace. Jesus is the Prince of Peace. He wants us to have the peace that surpasses all understanding. Perhaps you can even get a sense of His love just pouring through you.

As you sit here with Jesus, I want you to sense your mother coming into the room. She walks in slowly and moves over to the place where you and Jesus are sitting. For those of you who may not have known your mother, bring in a significant person in your life. Maybe it was a grandmother or an aunt or an older sister. But if you did know your mother, bring her in. As your mother comes toward you, she gently kneels down right in front of you and your eyes meet. As you look into her eyes, let Jesus still hold you, and hold you tightly, so that you can feel His love pouring into you and through you. As you look into your mother's eyes, begin to look with the eyes of Jesus. Look deep; look beyond the color. Look into her life. Look into her life where maybe you never dared to look before.

As you look, what do you see? Yes, maybe you see that she has hurts. There are hurts there that maybe you never knew anything about. There is pain. Maybe you are seeing that she had desires that were unfulfilled, desires that she never talked about. You can begin to understand that your parents were not perfect. Perhaps there were some imperfections in her because she did not have that perfect love from her father and mother. You can begin to see that she is a human being. She hurt like everybody else.

Now, as you look into her eyes, I want you to say something to her, as though, in reality, she is there before you. You can say it in a whisper. You can say it silently, but try to say to her, "Mother, I know that you were the best mother you could be, considering your background, your parents and your own life. I forgive you for any action, any thought, any deed that expressed less-than-perfect love for me. I forgive you for any hurt or any pain that ever was caused by your feelings."

Now, as you look at her, say to her, "Mother, as I forgive you, I ask you to forgive me. Forgive me, Mother, for not loving you with perfect love. Forgive me for not loving you as Jesus would have wanted me to, because I was imperfect too. Mother, forgive me for any time I ever felt angry toward you. Forgive me for holding all of those feelings against you when I felt that you rejected me, that you did not love me as much as you may have loved other people. Mother, I forgive you, and I give you the freedom to be a human being."

As you see your mother reaching out to you, she takes you into her arms. Go into her arms. Let your body feel that presence of her warmth, her love. As you are there within your mother's arms, we are going to ask Jesus, the divine Healer, to reach out. We are going to ask Jesus to place one hand upon your shoulder and one hand upon your mother's shoulder.

Lord Jesus Christ, we ask that You bridge the gap between the love we needed from each other and the love we gave each other. We thank You, Jesus, that right now in this moment, our relationship is being made totally whole, that it is being made completely healed, that You are becoming that perfect forgiveness between us – one to the other. We thank You that this relationship of child and mother has been perfected by Your love and by Your grace. In Your name we give thanks.

As you see your mother beginning to move back, look into her eyes and see that sense of peace and relief. The entire burden, all of the stress, has been removed by Jesus. Your mother has become a perfect mother through the grace of Jesus. All of her mistakes toward you have been redeemed through Jesus. She is happy and she is filled with joy. She waves good-bye to you and she walks out of the room. As you sit here now with Jesus and He holds you a little bit closer, you might feel a little emotion. This might not have been easy for you. Maybe you did not feel anything at all. That is alright; just sit here now with Jesus because He wants to bring your father into the room.

He wants to bring your dad in now so that you can experience total forgiveness and total healing in your relationship with your dad. Now as you sit here with Jesus, try to see your father coming into the room, walking toward you, coming closer until he is right there before you and Jesus. Maybe he looks a little bit confused. Maybe you have some emotion; maybe you do not want him there or maybe you feel nothing. Maybe you are happy to see him. Maybe you feel a little bit of joy. As your father walks closer, he comes over and kneels down before you and Jesus and as you look at your father, I want you to say something to him that may be very difficult. As you look at him, maybe you could recall how you always expected so much from your father. You always judged him when he did not live up to what you expected him to be. Maybe you feel he did not punish you justly. Maybe you feel he punished you too much. Maybe you feel he did not spend enough time with you. So say to your father, "Dad, I forgive you for every mistake that you ever made. I give you the freedom to be an imperfect human being. I give you the freedom to have made every single mistake in my life that you did because I know now that you were the best dad that you could be under the circumstances of your life."

Now look at your father. You do not have to think back to all the negative moments in your life but just say, "Dad" or "Daddy, forgive me for all the things I should have done for you and I did not do. Forgive me for holding any grudge against you. Forgive me for demanding more of you than you could be. Forgive me for holding things in bitterness and resentment. I love you." See him now reach his arms out to you and go right into his arms. There may be some of you feeling all kinds of emotions right now. Perhaps you do not want to go into his arms. Maybe you are happy just to be immersed in his love.

We are going to ask Jesus now to come and heal every emotion you are experiencing. Maybe you did not mean it when you said, "I love you." We are going to ask Jesus to honor Your words of obedience when He says, "Love one another." So, Lord Jesus Christ, we ask that You lay one hand upon this child that we are and that You lay the other hand upon our father. Jesus, only You know every experience; only You know every moment of hostility, every moment of love that has ever been transmitted from one person to the other. So, Lord Jesus, we ask that You move through the power of the Holy Spirit into every moment, every experience these two have shared and that You, Lord, become perfect forgiveness, that You become that perfect love, that You consume any negative feelings or emotions that are deeply repressed, that You bridge the gap between the perfect love that these two needed from each other and the love they were able to give. We thank You, Jesus, that it is by Your grace that this relationship is healed.

It is through Your unconditional love that our father's mistakes and our mistakes can be redeemed. Lord, we thank You that You are the divine Healer, the one who is perfect forgiveness.

Now, as you look into your father's eyes, you see nothing but joy; you see nothing but a healed person, a person who has been set free, a person who has been freed from all the burdens of guilt, oppression and imperfection. Your father joyfully walks out of the room and leaves you here with Jesus. As you sit here, you know that Jesus has performed a tremendous healing in your life. Jesus has just opened the way for you so that you are going to be able to move into a deeper relationship with your heavenly Father because these old bondages have been removed.

Remember that inner healing is a process. This is a prayer that you may have to pray continuously over and over because every level of unforgiveness has to be healed in our lives, not only toward our mothers and our fathers but toward every significant person; every relationship in our lives has to be healed through forgiveness. All we have to do is to close our eyes, bring Jesus into the situation and begin to bring before us those we have hurt and caused pain, as well as those who have hurt us. Allow Jesus to be the one who is perfect forgiveness in that relationship.

Lord, help us to realize that there is meaning in everything that happens. Fill us with Your compassion when others hurt us so that, rather than hurting them back, we may see them with a new gentleness, for You tell us, Lord, to be compassionate as our Father in heaven is compassionate. You tell us not to judge and we will not be judged, not to condemn and we will not be condemned, to grant pardon and we will be forgiven too. Thank You, Jesus, for letting us know that You are truly the gift of God's free love to us,

His forgiving, redeeming, sanctifying love, and that all of us are truly precious in Your sight.

The First Luminous Mystery:
The Baptism in the Jordan

Let us now revisit the baptism of Jesus in the river. Close your eyes and gently allow the Holy Spirit to bring you into a deep stillness within your heart. Relax and rest. Seek the interior silence with your mind, your heart, your soul, your strength, and become completely open to the Holy Spirit's anointing.

Now, imagine that you and other people are walking by the river and you see a big crowd of people gathered along the river there. You are drawn to move closer to see what is going on. You see a man baptizing – the young, the old, men, women, children. As you look closely at him, you notice the holiness coming through him and you ask someone in the crowd, "Who is this man?" People start to tell you, "His name is John, and he is a messenger of the Lord."

You look at him again and you are amazed at how people are drawn to him. He is pouring water upon each person. As he does, there is a change in each one's face. You see a sense of relief, a sense of freedom, a sense of peace in each person.

Then, another man comes up to John. There is something quite different about Him. You ask again, "Who is this man approaching John?" And someone replies, "Oh, He is Jesus, the Nazarene." You notice that Jesus' eyes are full of love and His presence is filled with great peace, a peace that seems to surpass understanding.

He too asks John to baptize Him, but when their eyes meet, you can see that John knows something about Jesus and he hesitates to baptize Him at first. But Jesus bows down and waits for John to pour out water upon Him because, for now, it is the Father's will. So without a word, John draws abundant water from the river and obediently baptizes Jesus.

Suddenly, the heavens open and the Holy Spirit descends on Jesus in the form of a dove. Then a voice from heaven is heard: "You are my beloved Son. On you my favor rests." The whole place becomes still and the voice of God echoes in your heart. You feel a deep longing in your soul to approach Jesus. And so, you now go to Him in haste with courage and faith. The water is still dripping from His body when He catches sight of you and looks into your eyes with tenderness, mercy, and grace. As He gazes at you, you can see that He knows the desires of your heart. He motions for you to come into the water and, without hesitation, you obey Him. Before a word comes out of your lips, light comes through Him into your heart and peace begins to flow like a river deep within. It is a moment of truth – a moment of truth and of time. You are encountering the Son of the living God, who is in your midst, who is here **now** in our midst. It is a moment of intimacy that He alone can reveal to a heart that is thirsting for true love.

He lovingly touches you now and draws you close to Him. With unspeakable joy He says, "No one can see the kingdom of God without being born from above. You must all be begotten from above. My child, the kingdom of God is yours. Be filled now with the Holy Spirit and receive the gift of life."

You begin to experience more fully, more deeply, the power of God's love penetrating your inmost being. That new life and birth is being given to the child within. Let your heart hear God's gentle voice saying, "You too, are My beloved

child in whom I am well pleased and upon whom My Spirit
rests."

The Second Luminous Mystery:
The Wedding Feast at Cana

As we continue to receive the keys to God's kingdom, we will again ask the Holy Spirit to reset a Scriptural scene for us. This time, we want to look at this beautiful mystery of the Wedding Feast of Cana. Let us ask the Holy Spirit to touch our imaginations and to prepare our hearts to encounter the living God with the help of Mary, our Mother.

Close your eyes and just let the Spirit minister to you. In your imagination, see if you can find yourself as one of the servers in this beautiful celebration. You listen to the festive music and you watch the merry dancing. You hear the laughter of the guests and serve the food and wine from table to table. You notice the glow in the bride's face while the bridegroom is intently gazing at her when you walk by them. Many family members and friends share in their joy.

Suddenly, your eyes catch the table where Jesus and His friends are seated. They are truly enjoying themselves as well. You are drawn by their fellowship and you watch them with fascination. Then, Mary, the Mother of Jesus, goes to Him and says, "They have no wine." You hear Jesus answer her, "Woman, how does your concern affect me? My hour has not yet come."

Now at first, you are startled by their conversation. But Jesus' mother looks at Him with such tenderness and yet with so much confidence that you understand that Jesus will heed her request. As Jesus glances back at His mother, you can see that He knows what is in her heart. Mary tells you and all the other servers, "Do whatever he tells you." Then she leaves quietly and goes back to her seat. You are surprised by what you hear and you keep looking at her. She displays sincerity, simplicity, humility, and a motherly love that you have not encountered before. But, most of all, you realize that she knows, deeply, her son; and she knows that her son will not disappoint her.

Now, there are six stone water jars there for the Jewish ceremonial washings, each holding twenty to thirty gallons. Jesus, speaking in a calm voice, says to all of you, "Fill the jars with water." Without any question or hesitation, you are moved to fill each container to the brim. You hear the authority in His voice and yet you see gentleness abiding in His presence. Again Jesus speaks. "Draw some out now and take it to the head waiter." You obediently take it and give it to the head waiter. The head waiter tastes the water that has become wine without knowing where it came from, although **you** know about the miracle. You remain silent. The headwaiter calls the bridegroom and says to him, "Everyone serves the best wine first, then, when people have drunk freely, an inferior one. But, **you** have kept the best wine until now."

You are taken by what you have witnessed. A miracle has happened before your eyes. Water was changed into wine. As you ponder this, you cannot deny how the heart exchange between mother and son touched you. When it is your turn to taste the new wine, you know that this wine is not from natural grapes. Then, with a profound grace from the Holy Spirit, you understand that this is the fruit of Mary's docility and Jesus' humility. This is the new wine that will bring new life to the bride of Christ, the Church.

Now, ponder whether the jars within your heart are filled with old wine or new wine. Ask Jesus and Mary to show you how to seek God's kingship first, so that you can give to others what you receive.

Ask Jesus and Mary to obtain for you the gift of humility and make it part of your intercessory lifestyle. Remember the scripture in Matthew 23:11-12, "The greatest among you must be your servant. Whoever exalts himself will be humbled but whoever humbles himself will be exalted."

And though we have entered into this mystery of Cana, this mystery of love, as the servers, we are reminded by the Lord that He is in our midst as one who serves. He truly is here in our midst and asks us to allow Him to serve us as well.

In your imagination, allow Him to come right before you and to kneel before you, right where you are. Allow Him to kneel at your feet and hear Him say these words to you, "I have come to serve **you**. I want to serve you because then, in turn, I am going to send you out to serve others. So let me kneel before you and let me give you all that you need." God will never be outdone in generosity. When we seek Him first, His kingship, His authority, everything else will be given.

As He kneels here before you, He looks intently into your eyes and you look into His. He can see deep, deep, deep inside of you. He sees every moment of your life that you have ever lived. He sees all the heartache you have ever had. He sees all the joy. He sees back over the years. He sees all the times that you have been happy, that you have been loving, and generous. He also sees those times when you have been despondent, when you have felt that you were a failure. He sees all the blessings that you have had and He sees all the tears that you have shed.

As He looks deeper and deeper, He sees all of the loving things you have done, all the things that no one knows about except you – beautiful things in your life that you have always kept hidden.

You begin to realize that He knows – that He can see – deep down within how truly beautiful you are. You realize, too, that He sees those blocks, those negative aspects of your life that keep you from knowing what a beautiful person you really are. He sees the things that keep you from knowing that you are a loving person. And as He looks into your eyes, you can see that He loves you so much that He can't stand for these blocks to be there.

As He begins to pour His love into you, you feel almost as if He is a magnet. His love is so pure, so radiant, that the light that begins to come forth from Him starts to draw from you all the darkness that is within you. As He sees that darkness within you – specks of guilt, specks of rejection, maybe little dark spots of unforgiveness and broken relationships, specks of inferiority – He sees the times when you have been put down, criticized, judged and condemned. Slowly, as He kneels there before you, that darkness begins to be drawn from you. In your mind's eye you may even be able to sense that there is a stream of darkness pouring from you – out through your heart. As it begins to come out, it comes into the light of Jesus and is consumed in His light. Remember the Scripture that says, "...perfect love drives out fear" (1 Jn 4:18). It means that this perfect love diminishes your fear and consumes it. His perfect love consumes all guilt. His perfect love consumes all feelings of rejection, all self-hate, all hostility.

As He continues to kneel here, all of the little shadows of darkness begin to come out until it is no longer a dark stream that comes forth, but maybe lighter shades of gray. All the guilt begins to break loose. All the unforgiveness breaks loose. All the unloving actions begin to break loose and all of it flows from you, from the center of your being, from that deep heart level, that deep unconscious level. It flows out from you and is consumed in His perfect love.

Now, as you sit here you realize that you feel lighter, emptier and freer. No darkness, no pain, no guilt, no hurt is there. Jesus speaks to you, "This is why I have come, to set you free. I have come to make you a free person so that you can have joy overflowing and love overflowing all the time."

Now, as He draws this out, His love begins to move into you. The light from Jesus begins to fill every part of your being. There is that rushing of His love, that rushing of His light, going into every empty place, into every void within your life. Long has He waited for your coming home to Him. He is filling you to overflowing. Every cell in your whole being, every thought, not only in your conscious mind but in your deep, unconscious mind, is being immersed in His love. Every unconscious thought is being consumed and filled with perfect love. Jesus is making you whole. He is healing you now in every way. He speaks to you again, "Now that you have given yourself to Me, now that you have surrendered your life to Me, I want to be **in** you and I want **you** to be in **Me** as I am in the Father and the Father is in Me (see Jn 14:20). I want to be flesh of your flesh and bone of your bone. I want to be one with you from now throughout all eternity, forever and ever." As He finishes speaking to you, you realize that you are being filled with His love, and so you thank Him.

We truly thank You, Jesus, that You have brought and are bringing each of us to this place of total surrender; that nothing, nothing, nothing can ever separate us from this love that we are experiencing in this moment in You, nothing in heaven, nothing on earth, nothing in the past, nothing in the future can ever separate us from **this** love that we have from You, from the Father through You, Jesus, in the power of the Holy Spirit. To You, Lord, Savior of our lives, we give **all** the glory. Amen.

The Third Luminous Mystery:
The Proclamation of the Kingdom of God
(Bartimaeus)

This meditation is from the Scripture about the healing of the blind man. Blindness, oftentimes, is lack of faith and seeing is faith. We want to see. We want to be healed.

Get comfortable now. Close your eyes. We open our hearts to receive another key to God's kingdom. In Matthew 17:20, Jesus tells us, "Amen, I say to you, if you have faith the size of a mustard seed, you will say to this mountain, 'Move from here to there,' and it will move. Nothing will be impossible for you." The kingdom of God is at hand. The kingdom of God is at hand and those who believe know, as Mary was told, nothing – nothing - is impossible with God.

In this scene, Bartimaeus, the blind man, is sitting by the dusty roadside begging for his next meal. He is blind; he feels weak, poor, helpless, scared, discouraged, alone, unwanted, and perhaps he is sick and tired of this kind of life (Luke 18:35-43).

Now, put yourself in his shoes and feel all these deep pains, fears, weaknesses and sufferings within your heart. Perhaps it is easy to identify with him because right now, maybe you also feel weak, vulnerable, afraid, hopeless, confused, burdened and alone. But suddenly, there is a throng of people coming your way. The commotion awakens you within and as you ask what is going on because you cannot see, you hear that Jesus of Nazareth is about to pass by. More emotions are coming into your heart as you feel more people rushing into the scene and you hear how they want to see this Jesus.

As you hear people talk about Jesus, His words of wisdom, His miracles and works of wonder, you decide to ask someone to bring you to Him. But nobody hears you. They ignore you and they are busy following the crowd. So, out of your poverty, your humility, but also out of your deep faith, **you** call out the name of Jesus! You know He can help you in your present situation. You want Him to remove the blindness from your eyes, the darkness of despair, the fear, the unforgiveness, the confusion, and the rejection that you are feeling right now. You call out, "Jesus, Son of David, have pity on me!" Despite the scolding, the opposition, the discrimination you receive from people, you call His name all the more with a loud cry, "Jesus, Son of David, have pity on me!"

Jesus stops. He hears you. Jesus asks you to come. At that point, you do. You jump up and you make your way to Jesus. With so much gentleness and compassion, Jesus holds you by the hand and asks you, "What do you want Me to do for you?" Now remember, Jesus is speaking to a blind person.

Could He not see what you want? Instead, He asks you, right now, "What do you want Me to do for you?" And you reply, "I want to see. Please open the eyes of my heart, for I want to see and receive Your light. I want to see you. I want to see Your heart's desire. I want to experience Your truth and the freedom it brings."

Continue to present to Jesus your needs, one at a time, for He is here for you. "What is it you want Me to do for you?" Listen to His voice and open the eyes of your heart to see the warmth of His gaze and receive the tender mercy that flows from His Sacred Heart. You are not alone. Jesus is here to help you carry your cross. Trust Him. Believe in His mercy and goodness. Believe that He knows the deepest intention of your heart. Believe that He is your healer, your deliverer, your provider, your Messiah. He is here to embrace you as a little child and He comes to meet you where you are. Believe that He loves you just as you are. Let His love, His all-enduring love, His compassionate love, His gentle love wipe away all your fears, your years of pain and the guilt from all your sins. He is here to give you a future full of peace and of hope. Rest now in His presence and receive this gift of light.

The Third Luminous Mystery:
The Proclamation of the Kingdom of God
(The Pool of Bethesda)

The scene that we want to recall now is the one in which many people are gathered around the pool in the city of Jerusalem. This scene took place during a Jewish religious feast. This pool had five porches and it was called the pool of Bethesda (Jn 5:1-9).

There were many people there. Most were sick or injured. There were the blind, the lame, the paralyzed, and they were all waiting for the water to move. Every now and then an angel of the Lord went down into the pool and stirred up the water. Everyone knew that the first sick person to go down into the pool after the water was stirred was made well. For us, these waters are healing waters – spiritual waters. They are waters of the Spirit, Himself.

By the side of the pool was a man who had been sick for 38 years! Jesus saw him there and knew he had been there a long time. Jesus, knowing perfectly well what the man wanted, presents a question. Jesus wants to hear from **us**. The question this time to this sick man was, "Do you **want** to get well?" Obviously he did. Why else would he have even been there at the pool? But Jesus wanted to hear from him. He wants to hear from us, "Do you **want** to get well?" The sick man answered and said, "Sir, I do not have anybody here to put me in the pool when the water is stirred up. While I am trying to get in, somebody else gets there first." Jesus simply says, "Pick up your mat and walk." This is power, the power of Spirit, the Father, Jesus. "Pick up your mat and walk." And immediately the man got up. Immediately he was healed.

Now, in the inner silence, in the quietness, imagine this pool. Imagine the setting and that you have just witnessed this miracle. Try to see the place. What kind of a place is it? Is it clean? Is it large? Is it small? You might notice the architecture or the weather, the people. Let the whole scene come to life. How many people are there in your scene? What sort of people are they? How are they dressed? What are they doing? What kind of illnesses are they suffering from and what are they saying?

It is not enough just to observe the scene as though watching a movie. We need to participate in it. What are you doing there? Why have you come to this place? What are your feelings? Do you speak to anyone, and if so, to whom?

Now notice the man who was just healed. Where is he? How is he dressed? Is there anyone with him? You might walk up to him and say to him – anything. You might want to ask him, "What happened? How did you feel about it?" As you are speaking with him, you notice out of the corner of your eye that Jesus is also still in this place. Where does He go? How does He act? What do you think He is feeling as He observes this entire scene of sick people? What are you feeling now? Take time and dwell on the question, "Do **you** want to get well?" Do **you** want a miracle in your life?

Jesus now turns to you and He engages you in conversation. Take a moment to talk to Him about the miracle that has just taken place. Is there any sickness that you are suffering from – physical, emotional, spiritual? If so, speak to Jesus about it. What does Jesus have to say? Listen to His words to you. "Do **you** want to get well?" Do you really mean what you say when you ask to be healed? And, are you ready to accept all the consequences of a healing?

You have now arrived at a moment of grace. Do you believe that Jesus can cure you and that He wants to do so? Do you have the trust that this will happen? Let Him touch you now. Let Him lay His hands upon you and heal your anxieties, your fears, your loneliness, your rejections, your anger, any hurt of any kind, any pain. Remember, Jesus knows how to walk into hearts. He walked through locked doors Easter night. He knows how to come with His peace and His presence. He knows how to come into any area, any room in your heart that still may be locked and breathe His spirit upon you. He is the healer. He is Jesus.

Spend a little time now in quiet prayer in the company of Jesus and beg Him for that beautiful gift of faith so that you truly can say, "Yes, Lord, I **do** believe. I believe that all things, **all** things, are possible with you."

The Fourth Luminous Mystery:
The Transfiguration

We want to be part of this mystery. We want to be there at Tabor. Let us now read this Gospel (Mt 17:1-8):

"After six days Jesus took Peter, James, and John his brother, and led them up a high mountain by themselves. And he was transfigured before them; his face shone like the sun and his clothes became white as light. And behold, Moses and Elijah appeared to them, conversing with Him. Then Peter said to Jesus in reply, 'Lord, it is good that we are here. If you wish, I will make three tents here, one for you, one for Moses, and one for Elijah.' While he was still speaking, behold, a bright cloud cast a shadow over them, then from the cloud came a voice that said, 'This is my beloved Son, with whom I am well pleased; listen to him.' When the disciples heard this, they fell prostrate and were very much afraid. But Jesus came and touched them, saying, 'Rise, and do not be afraid.' And when the disciples raised their eyes, they saw no one else but Jesus alone."

We want to imagine ourselves being invited by Jesus now to accompany Him with Peter, James and John to the mountain. As I climb, I may consider in detail the difficulty I am undertaking, pausing frequently to observe the changing perspective of the terrain below. But as I reach the summit, I am aware of Jesus and the disciples as they quiet themselves in prayer and I too relax and enter into prayer. I contemplate Jesus in prayer as He enters deeply into communion with God. I see this union of love reflected in His face, His posture, and in His total being and I allow myself to absorb this glory of God in Jesus. I also become aware of the presence of Moses and Elijah and listen carefully to their conversation with Jesus.

As the event unfolds, I am drawn into Peter's excitement and I desire to remain here. What did Peter and his companions hear? What did they see? They saw Moses and Elijah, of course, speaking with Jesus about the necessity of Jesus' own exodus, about His imminent suffering, death, and glorification. They saw the prophets of the Jewish Scriptures depart and give way to the new hope held in following Jesus, and the disciples were privileged to receive a sustaining glimpse of the glory of Jesus' resurrection. They heard again the word spoken at Jesus' baptism: "You are my beloved Son" (Lk 3:22). The voice definitely confirmed the identity of Jesus as God's Son and as God's divinely elected suffering servant. Then, enveloped by the awesome cloud of God's presence, the disciples received the instruction: "Listen to him."

I too become aware of the cloud of God's presence enveloping all of us. I listen and am aware of my own feelings, my own response, as I hear addressed to me the words, "You are my beloved Son...listen to him." Let us spend a few moments here, in the presence, on the mountain in God's light in the silence. Any thoughts or feelings that might surface through this time, feel free to record them in your journal.

Mount Sinai

I would like to take us through another little meditation now of another mountain top – Mount Sinai, where God's law was given. God has laws and His very special law is His law of love. We need to seek God's way. We need to climb that mountain with Moses. We need to experience that fire of God's presence. It is a purifying fire so that our hearts can make that Passover of purification and see God, no matter where, and hear Him, no matter through whom He speaks.

Come into the presence of God right now. He is here in the silence. Lord, we ask that You silence right now any noise within us and draw us into the fire of Your love.

Put yourself in Moses' shoes right now at the base of the mountain. You might even start to smell the smoke from this fire. As you smell this smoke, there is a movement in your heart to climb the mountain. Then slowly, you see a pathway through this mountain and you start to climb one step at a time with anticipation, expectation and excitement. You begin to move quicker than ever because you can now see the burning bush. You can see the amazing fire turning from red into gold. You cannot wait to get closer and closer to this beautiful fire. Your heart beats more quickly until finally you reach the top of the mountain.

As you reach the top of the mountain, there is this overwhelming peace that comes upon you. There is a gentle, gentle nudging in your heart to move closer to the burning bush. Slowly, very slowly, you walk toward the burning bush and you are taken by the sweetness and fragrance of what you see and feel. But when you look again, you see that the burning bush has changed into a heart-shaped fire. It is pure love. All of a sudden, you can see light – a beautiful light that is inviting you to enter into this heart-shaped fire. Then a door opens up from this heart inviting you to enter in. So slowly you enter into this heart, into this consuming fire, and a flood of peace, love and warmth comes upon you more and more. Then there is silence, a deep silence that only your heart can understand. In this silence you begin to hear a heartbeat and you begin to pay attention to this throbbing sound until you realize that this heartbeat is beating as one with your own heart.

Now, feel the heartbeat. Listen to the heartbeat and know that you have entered into the Sacred Heart of Jesus, into that heart which says, "Come to me, into that heart that has said, 'But the plan of the Lord stands forever, wise designs through all generations'" (Ps 33:11).

Ask Jesus, "Lord what is in Your heart for me today? Jesus, why have You invited me to come into Your heart? What do You want me to learn and to know and to experience from Your heart?" Whatever comes to your mind, write it down in your journal and continue listening to His voice, to His living word. Continue to dialogue with Him and let Him fill you with His love and grace; for truly, the pure of heart, they shall see God.

The Fifth Luminous Mystery:
The Institution of the Eucharist

Close your eyes and just rest in the silence as we continue to enter into the rebuilding of God's kingdom – God's kingdom within.

Feel the air that you breathe. Allow the Breath of God, the Holy Spirit, to remove any tension in your body. Be still and let His grace flow to silence any distracting thoughts or emotions that might be coming to your mind and heart. Prayerfully recall the last time you participated in the Sacrifice of the Mass. Perhaps you can recall the songs that touched your heart or the prayers that made you one with the congregation. Recall the different moments of intimacy with God.

Recall how you listened to the Liturgy of the Word and received nourishment from the truth that was revealed. The living Word, Jesus, prepares your heart to experience Him and His true presence in the Eucharist. Remember the different gestures of the priest at the altar as he prepares the gifts of bread and wine. Be conscious of the reality that you are part of this offering, all that you are. With full confidence you believe that the Father of mercy accepts the sacrifice His Son and His Bride offer to Him. You look intently as the priest raises up the bread and then says, "Take this, all of you, and eat it. This is my body which will be given up for you." And then he elevates the cup and says, "Take this all of you and drink from it. This is the cup of my blood, the blood of the new and everlasting covenant. It will be shed for you and for all, so that sins may be forgiven. Do this in memory of me" (see Lk 22:14-20).

Suddenly, your eyes are drawn to the hands of the celebrant. You look closely and you see that His hands have the nail prints of Christ. Deep within you recognize it is the Lord, the High Priest Himself (Heb 4:14-15), making this offering as a pledge of His love for you and for the Father. Extreme joy and awe fill your whole being. Truly it is the Lord who offers the bread of life and the blood of the Lamb (Rev 12:11) for your redemption, and that of the whole world. He knows the kind of spiritual food you need to sustain you in your life's journey.

So, enter into this spiritual communion. Believe in His intimate love for you and receive His kingdom that is free from the corruption of sin and death. Let His body heal and transform your flesh and let His precious blood cleanse and renew your spirit.

Now you hear a familiar voice within saying, "Believe. Believe that you are flesh of My flesh. You are heart of My heart. Take courage; I need your body. I need your love. Will you feed My lambs (Jn 21:15)? Will you allow yourself to be blessed, broken, and given away for the sake of love?"

A deep conviction comes upon you when you hear His call. As you receive His word and presence, you become mindful of holding His mystical Body in your heart. You realize His word is true and that the Eucharist nourishes the Church through His and your unconditional "yes" to the Father's will.

You begin to ponder His heart-piercing from which blood and water cleanses and heals countless, countless family trees and generations. By His wounds, you too are being healed (1 Pet 2:24), for remember, His love covers a multitude of sins.

And so, we rest in His love, His healing love, and His presence. We rest in His beauty and with the eyes of faith, with the eyes of the heart, we look upon Him as the beautiful one that we truly have come to know and believe and adore.

Speak Lord, Your Servant Is Listening

Close your eyes and imagine yourself walking down the road to Emmaus. You might feel the stones under your feet. You might even smell the stifling dust. It was probably a very hot day. Maybe it is warm now for you because you are right under the noon sun. You are right under the glory spout.

Share with Jesus your strongest feelings or whatever is most on your mind. If you do not know what to share, perhaps just feel the tension in your body. What is your body saying? Is there stress? Is there fatigue? Is there fear or anger? Is there a desire to change? Is there a desire for more gratitude? Whatever your body, your emotions, your mind is revealing to you, that is what you need to share.

When you look into the eyes of Jesus just take in what He is saying to you from Scripture during a time when He or another felt the same way. Breathe in His response until your heart is burning with all that is in His heart. Spend a few minutes just taking in what He says to you until you can live out His reaction. Feel free to use your imagination.

Maybe you do not hear Him right now. Maybe you can just touch or feel His presence or experience His presence. Whatever way you can experience His presence, be comfortable with that way.

Write down in your journal what is in your heart and write down what Jesus' response is to you.

Speak, Lord. Speak but Your word, and I shall be healed.

The Healing of Memories

God remembers. Our Father is memory Himself. We must allow God to penetrate deeper and deeper within us. We want to allow that perfect love of God's Spirit to heal us now. Close your eyes and move into the beautiful posture of receiving His abundance, of receiving all that He has for us.

As you relax just breathe in the Holy Spirit. Think of the Holy Spirit as immersing you in His love. In your imagination, see if you can see the light of Jesus moving through your being, lighting every single area of darkness within you. Try to imagine that you are there, before Jesus. Perhaps you are kneeling before Him. Perhaps you are sitting there, or just standing there facing Him. Maybe you are confessing to Him an area in your life that comes to mind, an area of disobedience, an area in which you have been unloving, an area of broken relationships.

Then perhaps in your heart say to Jesus, "Lord, I know that You see the darkness that is in my life. I praise and give You thanks that Your light removes all darkness within me. I confess to You, Jesus, that there are things unknown in my life that need to be healed and I offer myself as a living sacrifice to You, that Your healing love and Your healing power may remove this darkness, may remove these negative attitudes and that You may become perfect forgiveness within my life. Jesus, I give You permission to bring to my memory any unconfessed sin within my life that I might make it right, not only before You, Lord, but also before my brothers and sisters if I have offended them in any way. I rejoice, Jesus, to know that You are my healer and that no matter how far I have strayed from You and no matter how far I have strayed from obedience to Your word, You love me and You forgive me with unconditional love. Jesus, as I confess my humanity to You, I receive Your love and Your forgiveness through the blood that was shed on the cross for me."

As you sit with your heart open to receive Jesus' love, be aware of others so that as the healing love comes into the center of your being, it will flow right through you to others.

Jesus, as You touch us, continue filling us with Your healing love. We know that the blocks and the barriers that separate us from this love are there because of the ties and knots and areas of bondage within, those ideas of self-condemnation that prevent us from knowing how much You really love us. Touch my mind, the mind that I think with, the mind that I listen with. Lord, if I have any conscious block about Your ability to heal, I ask that this block be removed. Jesus, if I have any doubt as to whether or not You love me, I ask that You consume every doubt and grant me perfect faith, that I may believe.

Lord, in this act of obedience, we affirm that You do love us and that You desire for us to be whole. We know that You desire us to love the Father. We know that You desire us to love one another; and Lord, we know it is Your greatest desire that we love ourselves. We ask in Your love for us, in order to help us to love and accept ourselves, that You touch the hurt within us, that You touch that pain, that disappointment of which we may not even be aware. Jesus, we ask that Your love flow through our deep mind and touch every conflict, every fear, every anxiety, move into every moment where there has been depression or is in depression now. Move into every relationship where there has been any imperfection. Jesus, we ask that You move back into that deep mind, into the privacy of that unknown world within and bring forgiveness to each one who has ever brought any darkness into my life. Reach out and touch them Lord and forgive them.

Jesus, we ask that You remove the guilt that has been caused by our disobedience. And Lord Jesus, we ask that You remove the guilt of every sexual experience that we may have had, the guilt of all of the desires we have had within our mind that were never fulfilled. Remove the guilt that we have had toward ourselves for our unforgiveness and remove all the guilt of all the barriers that we have allowed to build up between ourselves and any other human being. We thank You, Jesus, that Your healing love is here now moving into each one of these areas. Jesus, because we do not know where and when that sense of unworthiness entered into us, we do not understand why we have been unable to accept ourselves. We ask You, Jesus, to move back even further into those early years of our life. Lord, we know that our lack of self-acceptance goes back to the little child within us who we have so much trouble loving and accepting and really understanding. Jesus, we ask that as You heal us as adults, that You heal every part of the little child within us. Give us all, Lord, the heart of a child and the courage to follow it.

We bring the little child that we are to You and we ask forgiveness for all the times that we blamed that little child for the many things he or she has done. That little child was hurt so many times and no one ever knew it.

Take that little child within us into Your arms and whisper deep into our ear, "I love you!" We ask for a miracle of the Holy Spirit. We ask that Your words can penetrate beyond the ear into that deep unconscious part of us, so that the little child may truly know Your unconditional love. Jesus, we ask that we would now be integrated with that little child who is within us. We ask that we, as adults, may get to know our inner child, that we may get to understand each other, that we may have that communication of perfect love with no judgmental attitudes, no blame, no condemnation. We thank You, Jesus, for bridging the gap between the adult we are and the little child that is still hurting within. We thank You, Jesus, that You are the healer and that right now You are bringing us into total integration and total wholeness with the child that is within us. We thank You that we can truly find the child Jesus within our temple.

We affirm our confidence in Your love for us; we know that You will continue transforming each one of us until we have become restored to complete wholeness, an expression of perfect love, not only to our fellow man, not only to the Father but to ourselves.

We pray this today asking, Lord, for Your great gift of wisdom to come. We believe Your word when You said to James, "But if any of you lacks wisdom, he should ask God who gives to all generously and ungrudgingly, and he will be given it" (Jas 1:5). We ask You now for this wisdom, this gift of gifts, that it may come in its fullness.

The Healing Power of Surrender

Close your eyes. Become quiet and picture that beautiful Gospel scene of Jesus kneeling at the feet of Peter washing Peter's feet. At the last supper, Peter did not really know how to receive what Jesus was doing for him. Jesus had to remind him, "I am in the midst of you as one who serves. Let Me minister to you." Let Jesus come now and kneel before you. This might seem strange because we are used to kneeling before Him, but He is in our midst now as one who serves. He is saying, "Let Me minister to you." Just try to relax and breathe in the Holy Spirit. Breathe in God's perfect love. Let Jesus kneel right in front of you and say to you, "I have come to serve you. I want to serve you. Then I will be sending you out to serve others. Let Me kneel before you now and let Me give you all that you need."

As He kneels before you He looks into your eyes. You look into His. He sees deep, deep inside of you. He sees every moment of your life that you have ever lived. He sees all the heartaches that you have ever had and He sees all the joy. He sees back over the years. He sees all the times that you have been happy, that you have been loving, generous. He sees those times when you have felt despondent, when you have felt like a failure. He sees all the blessings that you have had. He sees all the tears that you have shed. As He looks deeper and deeper, He sees all of the loving things you have done, all the things that no one knows about except you, the beautiful things in your life that you have always kept hidden. He knows that you, deep down within, are a beautiful person.

But He sees those blocks, the negative aspects of your life that keep you from knowing what a beautiful person you are. He sees the things that keep you from believing that you are a loving person. Know that as He looks into your eyes, He loves you so much that He cannot stand for those blocks to be there. As He begins to pour His love into you, He is like a magnet. His love is so pure, so radiant, that His life, His light, begins to come forth from Him to draw from you all the darkness that is within you. As He sees that darkness within you, there are little specks of guilt, little specks of rejection, little dark spots of unforgiveness and broken relationships. He sees those dark specks of inferiority. He knows when you have been put down, criticized, judged and condemned.

Suddenly that darkness begins to be drawn from you; maybe in your mind's eye you can even sense that there is a stream of darkness pouring from you, out from your heart and into the light of Jesus. It begins to be consumed by His light. Perfect love casts out fear. It means that His perfect love will diminish this fear and consume it. His perfect love consumes all guilt. His perfect love consumes all feelings of rejection, all self-hate and all hostility. As He continues to kneel there, all of the little shadows of darkness begin to come out until it is no longer black streams that come forth but lighter shades of gray. All the guilt begins to break loose; all the unforgiveness breaks loose. All the unloving action begins to break loose and all of it flows from the center of your being, that deep heart level, that deep unconscious level – it flows out from you, consumed in His perfect love.

Now you may begin to feel lighter, emptier, and freer, with no darkness, no pain, no guilt, and no hurt. Jesus is saying, "This is why I have come – to set you free. I came to make you a free person so that you can have joy overflowing, love overflowing, all the time." Now as He is drawing this out and you begin to feel emptier, allow His love to move more and more into you. That light from Jesus begins to fill every part of your being. There is that rushing of His love, that rushing of His light going into every empty place, into every void in your life. Long has He waited for your coming home to Him. He is filling you. He is filling you to overflowing. Every cell in your whole being – throughout your entire heart and spirit – is being immersed in His love, every thought, not only in your conscious mind but in your deep sub-conscious mind. Let every unconscious thought be consumed and filled now with perfect love. Jesus is making you whole. He is healing you now in every way.

He is saying to you, "Now that you have given yourself to Me, now that you have surrendered your life to Me, I want to be in you and I want you to be in Me as I am in the Father and the Father is in Me. I want to be flesh of your flesh and bone of your bone, one with you from now throughout all eternity forever and ever. And now as you give Me your heart, I want you to receive Mine. As you have surrendered yourself to Me, I too surrender myself totally to you." We thank You, Jesus, that You have brought each of us to this place of total surrender and that nothing, nothing, nothing can ever separate us from this love that we are experiencing at this moment – nothing in heaven – nothing on earth. Nothing in the past and nothing in the future can ever separate us from this love that we have from the Father through You, Jesus, and in You, Jesus, because of You. We give You all the glory.

The Healing of My House

Know that you are loved and in the presence of God. What we would like to pray about today and allow God to touch in any way that He wants, concerns two people – two people that came into our lives from the very beginning, who brought us into this world and against whom we can hold many things in our unconscious minds – our mothers and our fathers.

Imagine right now that Jesus is right where you are. You might want to rest your head upon His shoulder. You might want to allow Him to put His arm around you. Know that He is your friend. As you sit with Him, start to experience in His presence security and peace. He is the Prince of Peace. He wants us to have the peace that surpasses all understanding. Maybe you can even get a sense of His love just pouring through you and into you right now.

As you sit there with Jesus, I want you to sense your mother coming into the room. She walks in slowly and she comes over to the place where you and Jesus are sitting. For those of you who may not have had a mother, bring in another significant woman in your life. Maybe it was a grandmother, an aunt, or an older sister. But if you did have a mother, bring her in. As your mother comes toward you, she gently kneels down before you so that you can look right into her eyes. Let Jesus still hold you. Let Him hold you real tight. Feel His love pouring into you and through you. As you look into your mother's eyes, begin to look with the eyes of Jesus. Deep. Deep. Look beyond the color of her eyes. Look into her life. Look into her life where maybe you never dared to look before. What do you see? Maybe you see that she has hurts. There are hurts there that maybe you never knew anything about. Maybe you see pain. Maybe you are seeing that she had desires that were unfulfilled, desires that she never talked about. Now you can begin to understand that your mother was not perfect. There were some imperfections in her because she did not have perfect love from her father and mother. You can begin to see that she is a human being. She hurt like everybody else. Now, as you look into her eyes, I want you to say something to her as though in reality she were here right now. You can say it in a whisper. You can say it silently. But try to say to her, "Mother, I know that you were the best mother that you could be considering your background, your parents and your life and I forgive you for any actions, any deeds that were of less-than-perfect love toward me. I forgive you for any hurt or any pain that was ever caused by your feelings." Now as you look at her I want you to say, "Mother, as I forgive you, I ask that you would forgive me. Forgive me for not loving you with perfect love. Forgive me for not loving you as Jesus would have had me love because I was imperfect too. Forgive me for any time I ever felt anger towards you. Forgive me for holding all of those feelings against you when I thought that you rejected me, that you did not love me as much as you may have loved other people. Mother, I forgive you for everything and I give you the freedom to be a human being."

Now as you see your mother reaching out to you, let her take you into her arms and go into her arms and let your body feel that presence of her warmth, her love. As you are there in your mother's arms, we are going to ask Jesus now, who is the divine Healer, to reach out. We are going to ask Jesus to place one hand upon your shoulder and one hand upon your mother's shoulder.

Lord Jesus, we ask You to bridge the gap between the love

we needed from each other and the love we gave each other, that right now, in this moment, our relationship be made totally whole, that it be made completely healed, that You become that perfect forgiveness between us. We thank You that this relationship between child and mother is being perfected by Your love and Your grace. In Your name, Lord, we give thanks.

Now as you see your mother beginning to move back, look into her eyes and see her peace and relief. All of the burden, all of the stress has been removed by Jesus. Your mother is becoming now, a perfect mother through the grace of Jesus. All of her mistakes toward you have been redeemed through Jesus. She is happy and filled with joy. She waves good-bye to you now and she walks out of the room.

And as you sit there with Jesus and He holds you a little bit closer, maybe you feel a little emotion. Maybe it wasn't too easy. Maybe you did not feel anything. That is all right. Just sit here now with Jesus because He wants to bring your father into the room. He wants to bring your dad in now so that you can experience total forgiveness and total healing in your relationship with your dad. As you sit here with Jesus, try to see your father coming into the room walking toward you, coming closer until he is right here before you and Jesus. Maybe he looks a little bit confused. Maybe you have some emotion. Maybe you don't want him there. Maybe you feel nothing. Maybe you are happy to see him. Maybe you feel a little bit of joy. As your father walks closer, he comes over and kneels down before you. He is kneeling now before you and Jesus. As you look at your father, I want you to say something to him that may be very difficult. As you look at him, maybe you could recall how you always expected so much from your father. You always judged him when he didn't live up to what you expected him to be. Maybe you feel that he did not punish

130

you justly. Maybe you felt that he punished you too much. Maybe you felt that he did not spend enough time with you. I want you to say to your father, "Dad, I forgive you for every mistake that you ever made. I give you the freedom to be an imperfect human being. I give you the freedom to have made every single mistake in my life that you did because I know now that you were the best dad that you could be under the circumstances of your life."

Now I want you to look at your father. You don't have to recall the negative feelings in your life. Just say to him, "Dad, forgive me for all the things I should have done for you but didn't. Forgive me for holding any grudge against you. Forgive me for demanding more of you than you could be. Forgive me for holding things in bitterness and resentment." Simply say to him, "I love you." See him now reach his arms out to you. Go right into his arms. Now you might be experiencing all kinds of feelings. Maybe you do not want to go into his arms. Maybe you are very happy to be immersed in his love. We are going to ask Jesus now to come and heal every emotion you are experiencing. Maybe you did not mean it when you said, "I love you."

We are going to honor, Lord, Your words of obedience when You tell us to love one another. So, Jesus, we ask that You lay one hand upon this child that we are and that You lay Your other hand upon our father. Jesus, only You know every experience; You know every moment of hostility, every moment of love that has ever been transmitted between us. So Jesus, we ask that You move, through the power of the Holy Spirit, into every moment, every experience that we have shared with You and that Your perfect forgiveness and perfect love may consume any negative feelings or emotions that are deeply repressed so that You bridge the gap now with Your perfect love that we need – between our father and ourselves. We thank You,

Jesus, for it is by Your grace that this relationship is healed. It is by Your unconditional love that our father's mistakes and our mistakes can be redeemed. Lord, we thank You for being the divine Healer, the one who is perfect forgiveness.

Now, as you look into your father's eyes, you see nothing but joy. You see nothing but a healed person – a person who has been set free, free from all the burdens of guilt and oppression and imperfection. Now, your father joyously walks out of the room and leaves you here with Jesus. As you sit here, know that Jesus has done, and continues to perform a tremendous healing in your life. Jesus has opened the way for you to be able to move into a deeper relationship with the heavenly Father because old bondages have been removed.

Remember that inner healing is a process and that there may be deeper and deeper levels of unforgiveness toward your father, toward your mother, toward every significant person, toward every relationship in your life. Remember that all you have to do is close your eyes and bring Jesus into the situation. Bring before you those who have hurt you and those to whom you have caused pain as well. Allow the perfect forgiveness to occur between the two of you. Rather than hurting back, we may see them with a new gentleness.

Lord, You tell us to be compassionate as our heavenly Father is compassionate, not to judge and we will not be judged, not to condemn and we will not be condemned, but to grant pardon so that we will be forgiven too. Thank You, Jesus, for letting us know that You are truly the gift of God's free love to us – His forgiving love, His redeeming love, His sanctifying love and that all of us, all of us are truly precious in Your sight. Dear Blessed Mother, Lady of Wisdom, Lady of all Nations, Holy Mary, Mother of God,

pray for us, all of us, now and at the hour of our death.
Amen.

Birthings of Hope

The Sacramental system of the Church is so beautiful, rich, and mysterious. The spirituality that God keeps revealing to all of us day after day after day is always new. He loves new things. "Behold, I make all things new" (Rev 21:5). Especially, He makes all of **us** new. That is the best of all. That is hope.

Now we will try to reflect on the new birthings of hope that, of course, come through the beautiful Gift of Piety, that fire of hope, through which you come alive in a deeper way burning within for love of the Father.

Quiet yourself now and just let God minister directly to you in any way He so chooses. "Heavenly Father, I ask now to re-experience the holy anointing I received at my baptism. Most of us were baptized as infants and do not remember the power of the Sacrament – the gateway to life in Your Spirit. Even those of us who were baptized as older children or adults do not realize that all of heaven rejoiced when we were initiated and became children of God and members of the mystical Body of Jesus. So Father, make us aware of this magnificent grace which we received as pure gift from You, our most loving Abba. May this reflection draw us into Your intimate life by sharing daily in the sonship of Jesus and the fellowship of the Holy Spirit so that we will obtain new birthings of hope for ourselves and for the Church."

I hold the words of Jesus in my heart from Matthew 19:14: "Let the children come to me. Do not prevent them for the kingdom of heaven belongs to such as these." Mother Mary, lead me into the presence of the Holy Trinity as you were led. I desire to experience the coming of the Father, the Son, and the Holy Spirit in my body, in my soul and in my spirit in a deeper, deeper way, like a little child who is open, vulnerable and longing to receive. I open my heart to this encounter.

As I quiet myself, I begin to experience the Blessed Trinity lovingly looking at me before I was baptized. This gaze is like light that draws me out of darkness. I understand the gift of life that God chooses to bestow on me and I become aware that I am at the beginning of a whole new adventure.

Blessed Mother, I feel your presence around me. I feel your faith and love assuring me. Where you are, Mary, the Spirit is. Where you are, He always is. And I hear Jesus asking, "What do you wish to receive?" I answer, "I wish to receive everything. I wish to receive the fullness of the Spirit, the fullness of the Holy Spirit." Jesus says, "John baptized with water. I baptize you with fire." I hear the voice of Jesus saying with authority and love, "I baptize you in the name of the Father and of the Son and of the Holy Spirit," and an outpouring of love runs through me. At this moment, I experience being totally immersed in the love of the Trinity and unspeakable joy floods my heart as grace upon grace fills me. No thought, no word, and no gesture can describe this blessing.

Then I sense the gate of heaven opening and welcoming me. Once again I hear Jesus saying, "I now anoint you with the oil of salvation. As I was anointed priest, prophet, and king, so may you live always as a member of My body, sharing My mission of hope." This oil gives me power and strength to live a holy life in, with, and through Him.

Then Jesus says, "You have become a new creation and have clothed yourself in Me." I am now offered a white garment. I sigh in awe as I savor the newness and purity within me and experience the entire Trinity in my heart. I feel Jesus touching my ears to open them to hear the voice of the Lord. Next, He touches my mouth to speak the words of life to the praise and glory of God the Father. Lastly I hear, "You 'have clothed yourselves with Christ'" (Gal 3:27).

I see Our Lady smiling at me. Tears are coming down from my eyes as I experience God's glory in being a renewed, refreshed child of God. And, Father, I thank You for communicating to me Your infinite and intimate love, for embracing me as your own just as I am.

"My child, this is your birth into hope which draws life from the resurrection of Jesus. This is your re-birth to an imperishable inheritance not capable of fading or defilement, which is kept in heaven for you. This is your birth to a salvation which I am revealing to you. Your rebirth has come not from a destructible seed, but from an indestructible seed through My living and enduring word. Believe that I cast out the power of Satan and the spirit of any evil from you. Believe in the truth that you belong to Me and with Me you have everything. Believe that I bring you into the splendor of My kingdom of light. I have called you out of darkness into My marvelous light. Believe that I make you a temple of glory as I send the Holy Spirit to dwell within you. Believe that I mark you with the sign of the cross leaving the imprint of My life in your soul. May this experience ignite the fire of hope within you so that nothing, nothing, nothing can overtake you. Yes, I seal you with My covenant love that surpasses all your understanding.

"Now, through the action of the Holy Spirit, I unleash powerfully within you the gifts of faith, hope, and love and all the gifts of the Spirit to help you become a true child of

God, docile, meek and dependent upon Me, your Father.

"I give you especially this Gift of Piety to guide you to love Me and to love others as your brothers and sisters in Jesus and become that spark that sets many, many, many hearts on fire. Freely drink of this sacred fountain of grace as you fully consent to be reborn and choose to receive the fullness of the Holy Spirit."

I give praise to the Father now, for His gracious anointing of the Spirit and His promise from the Book of Revelation that the victor shall go clothed in white and his name shall never be erased from the book of life, but will be acknowledged in the presence of the Father and His angels (Rev 3:5). This is our faith. This is our hope. This is the hope of the Church. Be proud to confess it in Christ Jesus, the Lord.

Visions of Hope

I have been a spiritual director for many years and most of our people at Bellwether are spiritual directors as well. We have noticed that Understanding seems to be the gift of the Holy Spirit that is most lacking in people's spiritual lives. It is such a deep gift of friendship. Have you ever had a close friend and, when you are speaking to them you say, "But you just do not understand what I am saying"? It is painful when, between people who love each other, we do not understand. It is painful for God. He wants so much for us to understand that He gives us a special gift to help us understand Him.

He said this in a little bit different way to Saint Margaret Mary. He said, "The thoughts of my heart are to all generations" (see Ps 33:11). Those are mystical thoughts. Those are very deep friendship-type of thoughts. The only way we can understand that heart to heart communication is through this beautiful Gift of Understanding. It is a mystical gift because it is about entering more into His heart, into His mind, into His mystery of love. It is gift.

It is interesting the way the Holy Spirit will come in with this Gift of Understanding. All of a sudden, so gently that you are hardly aware of it, there is a light. It is something you did not know or understand; then, all of a sudden, you understand it. Maybe you cannot communicate it to anyone because usually when the Spirit gives us this gift there aren't any words; but we understand it without words. My mind knows. My heart knows. I asked Him one time, "How do You do that?" And He said, "Well, let's just call it 'bright ideas.'" So that is what He does with this beautiful gift. Of course, He is the brightness. He is the light and He is the idea.

We get all the credit of course. That is how He is. He is so hidden. He is so humble but He shares His heart. He shares His mind with us so that we can come into this deeper relationship and understand. We can understand how much we are loved. We can understand how close He is. We certainly cannot figure out on our own what a Trinitarian God is—one God, three Persons. What in the world does that mean? And how can we comprehend that this Trinitarian God is living within us unless we have this gift? It is a beautiful gift.

When we received the Baptism of the Holy Spirit in the cloister, I really saw this gift come to the forefront. Suddenly, everyone was aware, aware, aware. That is how the gift works. You are aware of something you did not see before. This gift now is there. You see it. You understand. Have you ever said to anyone, "Oh, now I see"? You are really saying, "Oh, now I understand." That is what we are talking about here.

Let us ask Jesus to break open this deep mystery within all of us. He has to break it open. Remember, the disciples were on the road to Emmaus. Jesus opened their minds to all the Scriptures that pertained to Himself, but they knew Him in the breaking of the bread. We really begin to know Him when He breaks open our bread—that hidden manna— when He breaks open that word. He is the bread. He is the Word and when He breaks it open for us, we begin to understand the deeper mystery of whatever is there in the Scripture. It has levels, and levels, and more levels. It goes on and on and on. How deep is the ocean? Who knows how deep the thoughts of God are?

So, Lord Jesus, we just want to take this time to come into Your presence in a very special way. We want to thank You, Lord, for coming into our very, very imperfect world and identifying with our broken humanity that we also may be bread that is broken. We ask You now to open our minds to see Your visions of hope for each one of us. Bless us, Lord, with a profound experience of the fire of love in Your heart, that our hearts too will be set ablaze and burn with love.

Lord, You said in John 10:10, "I came so that they might have life and have it more abundantly." Please help us to desire and receive this abundant life that You have reserved for us. Grant us the grace to encounter You in a new way so that we may worship You in spirit and in truth. For You have said that the Father is seeking those who will worship Him in spirit and in truth (Jn 4:23-24).

We ask that You remove the blindness in our minds and the deafness in our hearts that prevent us from grasping the deep truths of who You are and who we are in You. We give You permission to come to us as You are and as You desire. Make us aware of any false perceptions we have of You so that we may cast them away. Many times we try to box You in because we do not know You with our hearts. Send forth Your Holy Spirit to guide and accompany us in this reflection as we ardently seek to know, to love, and to serve You. Come Holy Spirit; pour out the Gift of Understanding to open our spiritual eyes to see the revelations from the Eucharistic Heart of Jesus.

Imagine yourself on the shore looking at the vast sea. You find comfort in being in nature, especially as you listen to the sound of the waves that silences the noise within. You feel the water lapping over your bare feet and it feels refreshing to you. You seek serenity which the city life takes away from you.

As you walk the shore, you are deep in thought searching

the true meaning of life. You realize that having a lovely home, successful business ventures and many achievements in life are just not enough for you.

While walking, your heart aches and you feel a yearning for something. Yet you do not know what it is you are looking for. Then you stop walking as you see a sailboat up ahead on the shore. You hear someone playing a familiar tune but you cannot remember the lyrics of the song. Your curiosity leads you to go near so you can clearly hear the song. Now you recognize it as a song that you used to sing in Church. Memories begin to flash in your mind as you listen to the rest of the song. As the music stops, you see a man watching you. You feel embarrassed by being there and as you are about to walk away, he kindly says to you, "It is alright. You may stay and I can play another song for you." Like a little child, your eyes light up with approval as you sit across from him.

He humbly introduces himself and you do the same. When the music plays, your heart silently cries out to God. The lyrics are answering some of your questions while the song touches your soul. You realize that this is God's love song to His people and to you. It may remind you of what you learned in religion class—that the heavenly Father sent Jesus to tell the world of His love. As a child you thought that when the sun was out, God was smiling at you, and when the rain came, He was crying with you.

You begin to understand that maybe you have lost your childlike faith. The world offers many choices that snatch away the presence of God within.

After the song is over, the man reads from John 1:14, "And the Word became flesh and made His dwelling among us and we saw His glory, the glory as of the Father's only Son full of grace and truth." You can feel that there is fire in His heart as he speaks God's word to you. He makes you understand that the meaning of life can be found through a personal relationship with Jesus. He makes these remarks. "Jesus comes to us in many ways. He comes to us through other people, sometimes through those who are close to us, sometimes through strangers. He conveys His love to us through nature, through music, Scriptures, inspirations and thoughts of the heart. He also reveals His truth through unexpected events in our ordinary lives. When He comes, He gives us a new vision of hope because He wants us to seek more of His presence."

You are impressed by his understanding of the Scriptures and you can tell that he knows Jesus. Then you ask him, "When did **you** meet Jesus in this way?" He replies with sincerity, "It was during a very turbulent time in my life when I was starving for love and searching for answers in all the wrong places. One night I found my mother's Bible that was shelved in a corner of her room. I picked it up, turned the pages and read 1 Cor 2:9: 'What eye has not seen, and ear has not heard, and what has not entered the human heart, what God has prepared for those who love him.' Something pierced my heart and I said a prayer to help **me** understand this passage.

"My heart began burning within me. I realized I was spiritually blind and emotionally deaf because of the traumas and pain I had experienced in my life. That night, Jesus came to break my chains and preserve my soul. He made me remember the times He had been there for me. When I was broken and lost He came to me through a friend. When I needed some words of hope, He came to me through a song. When I was imprisoned by my fears, He came to me through a teacher. When I was grieving the loss of my child, He came to me through a priest. When I was in a bad car accident, He came to me through a paramedic. From then on, I have believed that He is the God who is with us. I understand this reality more and more whenever I reflect on His presence in prayer."

As the man speaks, you experience his faith-sharing with you which makes you understand that God is near. You thank him for sharing his story with you. Then he plays another song and it is time for you to go. But before you say goodbye, he insists that you take his Bible home and you accept it without hesitation.

As you drive back home, you reflect on what happened and your faith is revived. You decide to stop by a Church because something inside tells you to spend a little more time with Jesus. You enter a back door that leads directly to the Adoration Chapel. To your surprise, Jesus is exposed in the Blessed Sacrament and tears begin to well up in your eyes. As you kneel before Him, you hear Him whisper in your heart, "My little one, thank you for responding to My invitation to come. I have been waiting to speak to your heart. I came to you today through the man on the shore – through the Scriptures he read, through the songs he played and through the stories he shared. I also came to you through the lapping of the waves, through the fragrance of the sea, through the memories of the heart and through the graces I give you each moment. Now I am here in the Holy Eucharist, truly present in your midst to reveal to you the thoughts of My heart. I am here for those who have eyes to see and those who have ears to hear. I place the longing in your heart to seek me that I may give you the hidden manna to satisfy the hunger of your soul. I give you My peace which is beyond all understanding and it will stand guard over your heart and mind. I have never forgotten you because you are glorious in My eyes and I love you. I desire that your love for Me may more and more abound both in understanding and wealth of experience so that others may see and believe in My presence in, with and through you. I have no hands but yours, no feet but yours, no voice but yours and no body but yours."

At that moment a veil is lifted from your understanding and you see Jesus' light shining within you. Then, you recall when you first received Holy Communion. You realized that He kissed your heart and left the seal of His love. Most of all, you remember the promise you made to Jesus, that you would hold Him always in your heart. It is an awakening call that enlightens your mind and enlivens your heart to embrace daily this spiritual communion with Jesus. You are speechless as you savor the truth, the knowledge, and the joy of finding Jesus once again in His rightful place in the temple of your heart.

Journeys of Hope

Lord Jesus, we ask You to show us the way on our journey of hope, for like Abraham (Heb 11:8), we too have traveled in stages in our spiritual lives. We thank You for giving us different companions on the journey. We are grateful for the challenges that You allow in our lives; they purify and strengthen our love.

So, in the spirit of prayer, lead us into this interior garden that we may recapture the essence of our origin and our life history. Lord, through this Gift of Counsel, help us to reflect on the meaning of Your words in John 10:27-28, "My sheep hear my voice; I know them, and they follow me. I give them eternal life, and they shall never perish. No one can take them out of my hand."

Let this be a moment of truth and grace for us now as the Lord guides us in this reflection.

I find myself at an open gate and written on top of it are the words, "The Garden of Hope." From a short distance, I hear the birds chirping with joy and I sense the gentle movement of the breeze inviting me to enter in.

I walk into the garden with excitement in my heart. I look around at everything with wonder and awe, like a child. I chase the butterflies of different colors and sizes and I observe that they are full of life. I touch the flowers in full bloom. Some are as big as my face, almost smiling at me. As I smell them, I ask myself, "Could this be the odor of sanctity?" I stand at a tree filled with fruit and I pick one. I taste it and I find it very good. It is a foretaste of heaven. God has promised me that if I persevere, I shall eat from the tree of life that grows in His garden and His garden is within.

I feel the harmony in creation and I experience the rhythm of pure love surrounding me. In the center of this amazing place is a bench. So, I sit down to rest and to be in God's presence. Then I notice a book next to me and as I turn the first page, I read, "The Garden of Hope." Suddenly, there is a yearning in my heart to grasp the gift of hope in this lovely garden. So, the story begins, "In the beginning God created the Garden of Hope to reflect His glory. He wrapped it in heavenly mystery. He adorned it with His riches and beauty. It was the King's glorious castle that He gave to mere earthen vessels. He created man and woman to live in the Garden of Hope. He nourished them with His living word. He formed them with His Spirit in one accord and one day, a test took place in the Garden of Hope. The woman heeded the voice of the serpent. He said she would be like God and she desired to gain more wisdom.

She ignored God and misused her freedom. She and the man ate the forbidden fruit and this Original Sin brought them fear, pain, shame, and hate and their disobedience led them astray. They were sent away. But God's compassion restored the Garden of Hope. Once it was stolen by the cunning deceiver but it was later ransomed by the blood of the Lamb (Rev 7:14).

On the cross, Jesus gave His all. He saved man and bridged the fall. His light shone in the darkness. His zeal consumed man's sinfulness and He showed His children the way of holiness. In Him, you too are chosen and forgiven.

"My little lamb, come to Me heedfully. Listen. Listen that you may have life. I will renew with you My everlasting covenant. I promise if you follow the promptings of My Spirit, you will live in My embrace. I promise if you listen to My voice, you will receive blessings without measure. I promise if you keep My commandments you will rediscover the true treasure. If you meditate on My truths and draw counsel from My word, I promise you will set captives free. If you humbly offer your will to Me, your enemies will be scattered. I desire to counsel you each day so that you will always follow My way so that you will always be in union with Me.

"Receive with a hope-filled heart this Gift of Counsel to assist you on your journey. Let your mind be transformed and renewed that you may discern My perfect will. I anoint you with My word so that you obtain strength from Me in times of weakness. I anoint you with My sacrament of healing so that you find comfort in Me in times of spiritual and physical illness. I place you into the Immaculate Heart of Mary so that you find refuge in her in times of purification. Let her *fiat* inspire you to look at the horizon and send My word into action. Let your 'yes' be a beacon of light to renew the face of the earth. Let your 'yes' be a building block to rebuild, to construct My glorified Church. Let your 'yes' lead other souls to journey into the Garden of Hope so that they will see My sanctuary within their hearts. Let the healing embers of your hope glow through your every 'yes'. Simply **do** whatever I tell you so that this day you will be with Me in paradise."

Wings of Hope

Father, help us to be open, docile and vulnerable to the Holy Spirit. We ask You, Holy Spirit, to lead us into a new homecoming. Help us, Holy Spirit, to surrender to the tender embrace of the Father. Make us aware that He is the source of all goodness. Deepen our desire never to offend Him.

Help us to understand that our true vocation is to respond to His call to holiness because He so wants us to be holy simply because He is holy.

We ask You now, Holy Spirit, to assist us in examining our thoughts, our words and our actions in the light of His love and truth. Reveal to us all the sins we have committed against each Person of the Trinity, other people and ourselves. Show us any unconfessed sins, sins of omission, unholy habits, hidden faults that may be curtailing our freedom to be childlike, to be pure of heart, to be holy. We ponder Your words, Lord, in Matthew 9:11-13, "Those who are well do not need a physician, but the sick do. Go and learn the meaning of the words, 'I desire mercy, not sacrifice.' I did not come to call the righteous but sinners." So Lord, we claim these words with hope in our hearts that we are forgiven and that we have Your love power to forgive others as well.

Imagine that you are cleaning your home. You are sorting out old things to be thrown away to make room in the house. In the middle of this busy afternoon, you hear the doorbell ring. At first you may hesitate to open the door for it will take you away from your work. Besides, you look at how messy your living room is and you notice nothing is in order. You too, feel dirty from this cleaning job. So, a little tug of war takes place in your heart whether to answer the door or not. But the bell rings a second time and you force yourself to open it. You are so surprised when you see Jesus standing at your doorstep. You begin to panic and wonder whether you will let Him in. He smiles at you as He waits to be invited in.

After hesitating a moment, you welcome Him into the living room. Now you look at Him with great embarrassment because of the disorder in your house. You want to run away from the situation but there isn't anyplace to go. In your mind, you start to blame your roommate for not helping you clean the house. Next, you might blame yourself for not fixing the mess earlier. Then you blame Jesus for coming to your home at this time without notice. Feelings of shame and guilt that reflect the chaos you feel within overwhelm you. And now, childhood memories of rejection, abandonment, abuse, condemnation and lack of love from your own family, trusted friends and others surface one by one. You are revisiting every broken relationship you have encountered in the past. You also feel the absence of God in those difficult and painful moments. You feel alone, hopeless and afraid because no one heard your cry for help.

With anger in your voice, you blurt out to Jesus, "I am sick and tired of this mess. I do not want this kind of life." Then with deep compassion, He turns to you and says, "I, too, am sick and tired of this mess. This is the reason I am here – to help you clean it up. You do not have to carry these burdens on your own (see Matt 11:28-30). I want to remove them from you so you can be free." But you protest out of wounded pride by saying, "Well, I made wrong choices in the past, so I have to pay the price for them." Then guilt engulfs you again and you sob right next to Jesus. Without hesitation, Jesus takes your hand within

149

His hands and He asks you, "Will you trust Me? Will you forgive others for all that they did to you or did not do for you? Will you forgive yourself for not being good enough?"

As you ponder His questions, you feel comforted by His touch and notice His scars. Something inside of you starts to break open as you look at those scars. He gently whispers in your ear, "I understand your troubles because I, too, hurt when you hurt. I, too, feel violated when you are violated. I am here right now in your heart crying with you. However, I cannot stop people from hurting you because of their free will. Their wounds are deep too and they believe the lies of the enemy. They, too, are victims of the sin and ill-treatment of other people. I am here now to set things right within you. Will you let Me ease your pain and heal your wounds?"

Then streams of light from His heart begin to fill your heart and you humbly answer, "My Lord and my savior, heal me. Forgive my sins and renew my life." You slowly lift your face up to look into His eyes and then you notice that there are tears in His eyes which heal your many years of pain.

Next, you watch a drop of blood come down from His forehead that reminds you of His crown of thorns. He speaks with such compassion to you, "I do not blame you for locking the door of your heart so tightly because you wanted to protect yourself. I am here for you and I want to draw the child within you out of fear, out of discouragement, out of unforgiveness. I want to shatter the lies that are embedded in your memories so that you will find treasures out of the darkness (see Is 45:3) and obtain riches that are hidden away. I brush away your offenses like a cloud, your sins like mist. Return to Me, for I have redeemed you by My blood on the cross. I want your spirit to soar on the wings of hope and find freedom through the Gift of the Fear of the Lord. I entrust the child within you to the maternal care of My Virgin Mother Mary and My tender loving Father."

You close your eyes and take refuge in Jesus' arms. Then the barriers within your heart melt away like wax. The burdens lift from your chest and tremendous peace floods your whole being as you receive every truth He reveals to you. Your whole house is filled with light and a fresh wind blows into it. When you open your eyes, you see the entire living room in complete order. You can go from room to room now and everything looks brand new. It is a miracle! You feel like a new creation from the inside out. Then, with excitement in His voice, Jesus says, "See, I make all things new (see Rev 21:3-5). I come to cleanse your temple with My tears and blood so that My joy may be yours and the Father's joy may be complete" (see Jn 15:11).

You remain in awe, in wonder, in the mystery, in joy and in peace as you continue to worship Him in your heart.

And so, Father, I thank You for Your unconditional love. I thank You that You sent Jesus. I thank You that You continue to send Him into my worldliness, into my world that is not Yours. I thank You for sending Jesus into this temple that is Yours to cleanse this temple from within.

Father, fill my soul with childlike hope and the desire to always reverence and serve You. And in gratitude for Your gift of Jesus' death on the cross, a death that took place because You so loved the world that You gave Your only Son (Jn 3:16) for me, I wish to respond fully to Your Holy Spirit who empowers me to be Your flaming arrow of reconciliation. I pray to keep Your ways until the end and receive Your authority over the nations, the very same authority that Jesus received from You because we are born in royalty.

I pray this today with great expectancy, love, and gratitude in Jesus' name. Amen.

Strengthenings of Hope

Lord Jesus, we come before You to re-experience now the reality of the graces we have received in the Sacrament of Confirmation. We desire to know the power of this sacrament as we reflect on the way You taught, Lord, in the synagogues after You returned in the power of the Spirit.

We also desire to be able to draw from the Gift of Fortitude the strength that our hope will need in the time of the trials and persecutions that are ahead in this turbulent night that our Holy Father has warned us about.

And so, as we enter into this meditation, we humbly ask the Holy Spirit to help us prayerfully use our imagination now as we place ourselves in the synagogue with Jesus.

So ask the Holy Spirit to calm your thoughts and let your mind follow His leading as He guides You in this meditation. Ask for an open heart.

Imagine yourself in the synagogue. It is the Sabbath. The room is crowded with people and there is something in the air that creates expectation. Many are waiting for Jesus, the son of Joseph, a carpenter from a town called Nazareth. Word is spreading that something unusual happened to Jesus when John baptized Him in the Jordan.

So when Jesus enters the place everyone starts to look at Him. He takes His seat, which is not too far from you. As you look at Him, you know there is something special about Him. You witnessed what happened when He was baptized in the Jordan.

In a little while, Jesus stands up to read and the attendant hands Him the scroll of the prophet Isaiah. The people watch closely as He unrolls the scroll. Then He proclaims, "The Spirit of the Lord is upon me because he has anointed me to bring glad tidings to the poor. He has sent me to proclaim liberty to captives and recovery of sight to the blind, to let the oppressed go free and to proclaim a year acceptable to the Lord" (Lk 4:18). He is a messenger of hope. There is a deep silence when He reads the passage and you can hear the authority in His voice.

All in the synagogue look intently at Him as He addresses everyone with these words, "Today, this Scripture passage is fulfilled in your hearing." As you listen to Him, His words become alive and give you hope. Everyone is marveling at the appealing discourse which comes from His lips but later the tone of Jesus' message changes. It cuts like a knife into hearts for He convicts the crowd of the poor practice of their faith.

This time, as He speaks, the whole audience becomes indignant. You hear judgment from the people's voices and you see anger in their actions. Next you are surprised by how they expel Him from the synagogue and they even lead Him to the brow of the hill to hurl Him down over the edge. Yet, He comes straight through the midst of the crowd and walks away.

There is profound sadness within you as you watch them reject and persecute Him. Something in your heart tells you to follow Him. Not minding the crowd, you begin to follow Him and before long He stops and asks, "What do you want from Me?" And you reply, "Lord, I heard You speak and I know what You say is true." He then asks, "Did you not see how they threw Me out of the synagogue? Did you not hear how they despise My words and still you want to follow Me?" And you respond, "I do. I want to be Your follower because I know You are a man of God. I believe You are a prophet and there is something more than my natural eyes can see. I want to learn from You the deep things of God."

Jesus looks at you lovingly and He inquires, "Have you been baptized?" You answer, "John baptized me in water, but I desire that you anoint me in the Holy Spirit." Without hesitation, Jesus lays His hands gently on your forehead and oil oozes from His palms; it soaks your head and you feel the warmth of His hands. The Holy Spirit's presence flows into your whole being. Then you hear Him say, "Be sealed with the gift of the Holy Spirit (see 2 Cor 1:22) and peace be to you."

Tears of joy roll down your face like open floodgates and awe overtakes you. He quickly embraces you with tenderness and beckons you to follow Him. You follow Him from village to village including the pagan territories. You listen to Him preach the word of God with boldness. He challenges the Pharisees, the Sadducees and other religious authorities without fear. You watch Him heal the sick, expel demons, give sight to the blind, cure lepers, and work other miracles. Truly He is filled with the Spirit of God and power gushes forth from Him.

But the more His name becomes known, the more enemies He gains. They are after His life and He is aware of the intense battle. But, even the threats on His life do not stop Him from going to Jerusalem.

One day the people exalt Him like a king as He enters triumphantly into the city riding on a donkey. But the next time they crucify Him on the cross. You find yourself at the foot of the cross gazing at Him whom you learned to love. Many things about Him linger in your heart that show you

He truly is the Son of God. You see the mercy and compassion of Jesus toward the people who led Him to Calvary. Truly He is the Lamb of God who takes away the sin of the world, for the Lord laid upon Him the guilt of all (Is 53:5-6).

At Calvary you experience His heart burning like a torch, filled with zeal for the Father's will, and you recall His words, "I have told you this so that you might have peace in me. In the world you will have trouble, but take courage, I have conquered the world" (Jn 16:33). You realize that to follow Jesus is to carry the cross with the same love and fortitude as He did.

He was and still is a sign of contradiction to a world of confusion. His teachings were and still are too much for many because He calls people to live in humility, obedience and self-emptying love. Yet He always promises good for us if we remain faithful. He will give us the crown of life and the victorious shall never be harmed by the second death (Rev 2:10-11).

You are encouraged. You hear Jesus say right now, "My little one, savor the light of truth you receive from this experience. Desire to know the depths of the reign of the Father's kingdom within your heart. The Holy Spirit overshadowed Mary and conceived Me in her womb so that I could do the Father's will. As I break open this mystery to you, believe in your true identity as a child of the King. I invite you now to share in My mission to bring God's love to all. I give you My Spirit to empower you to suffer and fight for My kingdom. Truly the Sacrament of Confirmation makes you a soldier of Christ. You are in My army of love. Spread and defend the faith through a life of courage, hope, and fortitude. There will be many obstacles and battles, but your victory is assured. Do not be weary but run with a burning desire to live the gospel without compromise. Be My fire of hope today. Today I am passing on to you the torch of freedom. Run the race to win and know that I am with you always so that we can triumph in our battle against the powers of darkness."

O Lord, I hear the urgency of the times. I believe that the spiritual battle has intensified in my own life and in the world. The consequences of sin and evil in the world are deadly and the standards of our society are truly in opposition to Your promise. The choice to enter the narrow gate (Matt 7:13) and to suffer for Your sake is not always easy because of my human weakness and many times the burden of sin pierces my heart because I know how much it hurts You.

Help me to lay myself down more fully so that I can join You on the altar of sacrifice for the salvation of souls. I truly believe, I believe, I believe Lord, that I am able to do all things in You and only in You, Who strengthens me (see Phil 4:13). I claim the graces I receive in the Sacrament of Confirmation, especially this Gift of Fortitude so that in my own flesh, I can now fill up what is still lacking to Your sufferings for the sake of Your Body, the Church.

Let us pray the prayer of St. Ignatius of Loyola:
"Dearest Lord, teach me to be generous. Teach me to serve you as you deserve, to give and not to count the cost, to fight and not to heed the wounds, to toil and not to seek for rest, to labor and not to ask for reward save that of knowing I am doing your will. Amen."

Promises of Hope

Today, let us ask our Blessed Mother to accompany us in this reflection:

"Dear Blessed Mother, please take us into your Immaculate Heart so that we may receive a fresh outpouring of this Gift of Knowledge so that we may know that we know that we know. Together with the Holy Spirit, guide us to fervently desire a spousal union with the Holy Trinity, with the Father, with Jesus, and the Holy Spirit.

Mother Mary, you are Mediatrix of all graces and we ask you today to please intercede for us that we, as Paul prayed, may grasp fully the breadth, the length, the height, and the depth of this Trinitarian love to experience this love which truly surpasses all understanding so that we may attain to the fullness of God Himself.

Show us, dear Blessed Mother, the countless treasures that the Holy Spirit shares with you so that we may know His promises and give our all to Him."

Imagine yourself now walking through a meadow on a lovely day. You watch the green grass standing tall. Colorful wildflowers are shimmering in the rays of the sun. You look above and see the beautiful blue sky. The wind is blowing gently upon your face and you smell the freshness of the field.

Then your senses open up to search the meaning of all the beauty and the loveliness of God's creation and you are drawn to how paradise must have been. At the end of the meadow, you see a hill and in haste you approach it. But before you climb, you see a cave that seems lit from inside.

You slowly walk toward the mouth of the cave and enter in. With astonishment, you see a beautiful lady standing in one corner of the cave and behind her are seven lamp stands. She does not seem surprised that you came. She welcomes you with a loving smile. You notice that the bright light that surrounds her is radiant but it does not blind your eyes. Instead, the light makes you recognize that it is the Blessed Mother waiting for you in this hidden, silent place.

Then she asks with enthusiasm, "What are you looking for, my dear one?" You truthfully reply, "I am searching for the deep meaning of God's love, of paradise regained." She motions you to come closer to her. Your heart jumps with joy as you approach her. She exudes childlike purity, true femininity, and motherly love altogether.

Then she gazes at you intently and very kindly says, "My little child, all this takes place within the cave of your heart. Whenever the soul of the Bride of Christ encounters Jesus, the divine Bridegroom in the solitude of the heart, she uncovers the beauty of intimate love. Whenever the soul turns away from self-love and turns towards God's desires within her heart, she grows closer to the source of all love.

"Whenever a soul resists the temptations of the devil and chooses to listen to God's voice in the heart, she experiences the rebirth of obedient love. Whenever the soul accepts the trials humbly and embraces the cross on the altar of her heart as a gift from God, she experiences the wonders of *agape* love."

So then you ponder a little what she has said and you tell her sincerely, "Mother Mary, show me more how to live in this paradise of loving union with the Beloved." Then you are amazed when you see that her Immaculate Heart is exposed before you. She walks you through her life and it

159

is like watching a movie in her heart.

She leads you to visit the annunciation of the angel and you recognize her listening, discerning and believing heart. At the visitation of Elizabeth, you capture her prophetic and obedient servant's heart (Lk 1:46-55). At the birth of Jesus, you experience her poor, humble and joyful heart. At the presentation of Jesus in the temple, you know her meek, selfless and grateful heart. When she finds Jesus in the temple, you understand her patient, understanding and compassionate heart. At Nazareth, you realize her silent, receptive and virtuous heart.

At Calvary, you capture her surrendered, sorrowful, and merciful heart (Jn 19:26-27). At the resurrection of Jesus, you experience her trusting, hope-filled and triumphant heart. At Pentecost, you understand her prayer and her zealous and grace-filled heart (Acts 1:14). Lastly, you know her undivided, sinless, and faithful heart, the heart which is always lovingly united to her Bridegroom.

This time you speak to her with a little doubt in your voice, "Mother Mary, you are full of grace, and I am not. It will take a miracle to follow the examples of your heart. Sometimes I feel that I take one step forward and two steps backward. How can this be?" Then she answers you encouragingly, "My little heart, you are the child of the King. You are the bride of the Lamb. You are the temple of the Holy Spirit. You are the Holy Trinity's priceless possession. You belong to Him and with God all things are possible. Jesus consecrated Himself for your sake on the cross. He prayed that all may be one in the love of the Trinity. Trust that His grace is sufficient for you (2 Cor 12:9) and continue to pray and strive to follow His ways."

When Our Lady finishes speaking, the Holy Spirit, as a pure

dove, flies out of her Immaculate Heart and rests upon yours. A profound knowledge of His abiding love deeply awakens your soul. Then you hear Him say to you, "My beautiful one, remember that the dawn begins with streaks of light and not with an explosion of light. Savor every moment and be thankful for the little miracles of grace that come throughout the day. Notice the little changes. You have a little more kindness for one another, a little more patience in a difficult situation (Gal 5:22-23). You notice a little more compassion to the lost, and a little more hope in times of darkness. These are signs of growth and spiritual awakening. Realize that it is not the vision that changes, but the heart that carries it out with more of my love and power. For even in a small way, love is still love and brings the soul into closer union with the Beloved.

"Thus, I am calling you today to be My branded, wedded warriors, to be one with Me in My *agape* Calvary love, to bring hope to those who have not yet known My love."

Then, the Holy Spirit asks you a question. "Do you perceive and believe your destiny?" You hear the words of Hosea resound in your soul, "I will espouse you to me forever. I will espouse you in right and in justice, in love and in mercy. I will espouse you in fidelity and I promise you shall **know** the Lord" (see Hos 2:21-22).

You believe that the Bride must prepare for the wedding feast of the Lamb and be clothed in the armor of His love, in the armor of light. You receive the knowledge that the bride's destiny is transforming union with the Lamb. Now you hear the Lamb cry out, "Set Me as a seal on your heart for stern as death is love. Its flames are a blazing fire."

You listen to the citizens of heaven pray in one voice, "The Spirit and the Bride say, 'Come.' Let him who hears

161

answer, 'Come' (Rev 22:17). Let him who is thirsty come forward. Let all who desire it accept the gift of this life-giving water" (see Is 55:1).

In silent wonder, with joy in your heart and love in your soul, you hear the invitation, "Come, My friend. Come, My dearest friend. Come and drink deeply. Drink deeply now of love."

Power of Hope

I want to share with you a few little things that the Lord brought to my attention in my own prayer life. You need to know the enemy. We are the sword, aren't we? We have become that sword. We have become that beautiful, docile instrument in the Spirit's love, in the Spirit's movement. But we need to know who we are fighting. When are we going to use this sword? How is it going to be used?

The Lord brought my attention one time in prayer to the book of Genesis, to that famous scene of Adam and Eve in the garden and their dialogue with the serpent. He drew my attention to how very much Satan hates the Father. I had not really seen that for awhile but now I began to see that Satan was undermining the Father. Now I knew why Jesus (of all the ways He could have referred to Satan) called him the **father** of lies. Satan wants to be father. He wants to be God. He doesn't want to be like God. He wants to be God. He wants to be even greater than God, but especially as father.

It is little wonder that St. Ignatius and many of our mystics in the Church could say for the **greater** honor and glory of God. They saw the many ways in which Satan was undermining the Father. Jesus, all through the Scriptures, only talks about the Father – the "Father" this and the "Father" that. It is beautiful when you start meditating on what Jesus has said about the Father. It's the Father's greater honor and glory that Jesus is reinstating (1 Tim 1:17).

Eve believed the lie. Satan lies. If we are going to defeat him by the word of our testimony then our testimony must be the sword of the Spirit (Rev 12:11). It is a sword of truth, isn't it? This is how we allow the Spirit to use us. We believe truth. We think truth. We speak truth. We know truth. But, I want to point out how we really gained that territory. We will know the truth because it will always be in the life of Jesus somewhere.

It says very beautifully in Scripture that after Jesus is baptized (it's interesting that it is after He is baptized), He is full of the Holy Spirit, full of this truth and He was led by the Holy Spirit into the desert (Mt 4:1). It is in the desert, in our solitude and in our silence – it might even be in our very special prayer time every day – that we are going to encounter Satan, the father of lies. It might be in our thought life. It might be even in our prayer life. Surely, you know what I am talking about. This is where we meet him. This is where the big battle is won.

Listen to him speak to Jesus: If you are the Son of God, well then command these stones be turned into bread (Lk 4:3-4). That's a good thing, isn't it? Have you ever heard, "If you are a child of God, why don't you go and do this? Why don't you go and do that? You are a child of God. That is a good thing." Watch those good things. Is it God's will? That is all that counts.

Eve saw that that fruit was good and pleasing. It was good, but the Father had said, "Not for you. It is **no**." Satan lies. Is it good for me? Jesus said, "No. No." It is interesting what Jesus says: "'One does not live by bread alone, but by every word that comes forth from the mouth of God'" (Mt 4:4). That is how Jesus lived. That is how He is the sword. He lived by every word that came forth from the mouth of God, not the mouth of Satan.

We need tremendous discernment. We need light. This is why we need to be full of the Holy Spirit. This is who He

164

is. He is truth. He is light.

Look at the second thing that Satan says to Jesus: I will give you power and the glory of these kingdoms (Lk 4:5-8). You will be like gods (plural). I will give you kingdoms. This power has been given to me and I give it to whomever I will. Well, we know that the kingdom of Satan is here, isn't it? He has lots of kingdoms. Turn on the television. Go to the movies. Listen to almost anybody. The kingdom of Satan is everywhere. It is evil, evil, evil. It is lies, lies, lies. It is leading many, many, many astray, isn't it? It is all darkness. It's not truth (1 Jn 1:6).

Jesus has asked us to go to the Father for His kingdom. Father, the only kingdom I want is Your kingdom. Your kingdom come. Come right now in me. I do not want these other kingdoms.

We are called, too, to live in the world. The world has its own spirituality. But we are not called to be **of** it. There is another kingdom within us out of which we live. Jesus says, "No, no." Satan wants to be adored. "Adore me" is the condition for his kingdoms. "Adore me. Make me first in your life and it will all be yours." But Jesus says, "Adore God. Adore the Lord your God and him alone." Isn't that beautiful? Jesus cuts through the lies. As the swords of truth we must cut through the lies. Here is the third big lie: If you are the Son of God…. Look at all these "ifs": If you are a child of God…If you know God as you say…If you are so loved by God…If you really believe you are created in His image and His likeness…. It is going to be that "if, if, if" and he will use truth as well. There's always going to be an element of truth in what Satan says – If you are the Son of God… Well, Jesus was and is the Son of God. So this is where the temptation is great. Remember, even on the cross Jesus heard, "If you are the Son of God, come down off that cross." Jesus could have come down. It was not nails that held Him on that cross. It was love – love for the Father, the Father, the Father. That is who Satan hates more than anyone or anything.

So he says, "If you are the Son of God, throw yourself down for His angels will watch over you (see Lk 4:9-12). They will support you. You will never stumble." This sounds pretty good. "Throw yourself down. Trust God. He will uphold you. You will not fall into anymore mud puddles. You are going to make it." It sounds good, doesn't it? But Jesus said, "Do not put the Lord, your God, to the test." In other words, we do not presume.

Sometimes you can get into such a beautiful relationship that you presume, you assume that it is going to be alright with that person – whatever you do. That is a big mistake, isn't it? Jesus said, "Do not do that." Make **sure** it is alright with the Father. Seek the Father at all times.

I think it is good for us to know that this battle can begin within ourselves in desert spirituality in the silence and the solitude within. But when we can come against the lies, the lies, the lies that come in prayer and conquer them with truth, we are going to be able to use and to become that sword wherever we hear it and wherever we see it. The big battle has been won within and we ourselves know now, in a deeper way, who Satan is. We **know** how he is working. We hear him. You can maybe hear him coming through a person. You can hear him come through the news. You can hear him come through the media all the time. You can hear him come through a friend. You will know him. You will know him. You will know him just like you know God because you have spent time with God. That desert spirituality, that contemplative posture is where the light is. That is what will be revealed to us and we will truly know our enemy.

God said, "I formed you, and set you as a covenant of the people, a light for the nations..." (Is 42:6). We can be that light because we have the fullness of the Spirit and we allow the Spirit to use us with that light, with that truth. This truth, this light will engage us in the same mission with Jesus. It will open the eyes of the blind. We can get that light for them. It will set the captives free, free from the lies, free from the false bondage, free from what they think is going to make them happy, from what they **think** is going to be heaven.

With the Gift of Wisdom, we have God's eyesight. We have His binoculars. We might not be there fully, but we have hope because we can see. It is a reality. We can see a lot of things. "Come up here," He said. "Come up here into My presence. I will show you. I will show you. I will show you" (see Rev 4:1). That is wisdom. We need to see. We can see where the enemy is. We know where he is. We can cut through that lie and that darkness because we can see. We are not in the dark. We can proclaim liberty to captives because we know the truth. It is only truth, God's truth, that sets people free.

We need to know the Scriptures, don't we? We need to know what Jesus has said. That is truth. That Bible is written by God! Thus it is written! That is truth. Use it. Use it. It is your sword in a special way.

There are beautiful sayings in Revelation. One of the most beautiful promises is in Revelation 3:21, "I will give the victor the right to sit with me on my throne as I myself took my seat beside my Father on his throne." That is the power of intercession!

167

In Isaiah, there is another promise that goes with it: "I, the LORD, have called you for the victory of justice..." (42:6). I have called you for this victory! I have called you so you can have this kind of authority, this kind of power, this kind of vision at My right hand. That is the hand of power. He said, "Earlier things have come to pass and new ones, now, new ones I foretell. I am announcing them now to you" (Is 42:9). He is showing us new things, new things deep in the heart that come very much out of these beautiful seven Gifts of the Holy Spirit.

Maybe you have noticed there is a thread that connects all of God's gifts. It is the thread of dying. We are called to die so that He can live, so that the gifts can come forth fully. The wisdom gift is the epitome of dying, isn't it? Every "yes" to God is a "no" to me. Every "yes" means there is a "no" and the "no" is to my way, my opinion, my life, my preferences. Our response must always be, "Yes. Be it done according to your word" (see Lk 1:38). God's word is wisdom and it becomes incarnate within us with every "yes".

When I was in the cloister, He showed me something very, very beautiful. How can a little cloistered nun reach a world? Nobody can come into the cloister and we didn't go out. How are we going to reach a world? He showed me that it is the same way Our Lady did. With every "yes" we are coming into the spirituality of the priesthood as priestly people. A priest has the power of God to bring Jesus upon that altar and to give Him away as food, doesn't he? As priestly people, our "yes" brings Jesus upon the altar of our hearts and it can bring Jesus upon the altar of all hearts. Isn't that beautiful? It is our "yes" that allows Jesus to be reborn again in heart after heart after heart. That is wisdom.

Wisdom can become incarnated again in body after body

after body through, maybe, one person's little "yes". Can you imagine what He can do with a room full of "yeses"? We get the whole world!

So, it is exciting! We are called to die so that wisdom and these beautiful gifts of life can flow. It is good to remember that it all comes from the pierced heart of Jesus. But maybe, sometimes we forget that when the heart of Jesus was pierced, He was already dead. When we are really "dead" then look at what can flow out from our hearts. It is pure God; it is pure love; it is pure life for others. That is the lifestyle to which we are called. That is the mission of Jesus Christ, the Lamb of God who continues to take away the sin of the world in, with and through us.

Our prayer today is that God will really make us again a very contemplative Church, a prayerful Church and that He will continue to raise up a priesthood in union with His crucified, pierced heart. It is a sacrificial lifestyle as priestly people for all of us but the reward is great. It is new life for others and there is no joy like seeing a baby born, is there? We are going to see a baby born and we are going to see it soon. It is going to be Jesus. We already know His name. He shall be called Jesus.

Publications from
The Intercessors of the Lamb

Books

God's Armor
Teachings on St. Paul's letter to the Ephesians 6:10-18.
Everything about the armor, everything we need to grow
and to be nurtured and strengthened, everything in which
we must be clothed comes from Heaven.
Discover the power and strength of the Armor of God.

Interceding with Jesus
"I have searched among them for someone who could build
a wall or stand in the breach before me to keep me from
destroying the land; but I found no one" (Ez 22:30).
Discover what it means to stand in the breach, to become a
burden-bearer for the Lord.

Bathe Seven Times
Our number one best seller, now being used world wide in
monasteries, seminaries, convents and homes, offers a
contemplative look at the seven capital sins, their roots and
the surprising places in which they conceal themselves in
our lives.

Heart Whisperings from the Desert
Discover the fruits of contemplative listening.
Poetry and Prose from the Hermit Community of the
Intercessors of the Lamb.

Inner Healing through the Heart of Jesus
Deep insight into the powerful impact of turning to Christ for the healing of our memory, our intellect and ultimately, our will.

Spiritual Direction
in the Footsteps of the Shepherd
Practical teachings on authentic spiritual direction. Excellent suggestions will help the reader experience effective spiritual direction both as a director and as a directee. Includes an appendix with more than 20 inner healing meditations and prayer reflections.

Feed My Lambs Series
Nourish your spiritual life with readings for every week of the year. Feed My Lambs *is a series that features powerful meditations and teachings geared to help intercessors live their faith more vibrantly, and ultimately, to grow more deeply in their relationship with the Trinity.*

Formation Study Series

Empowerment of the Holy Spirit
Heart to Heart Listening
Hearing God's Voice
Prayer Warrior Summit (The Seven Capital Sins)
Our Father
Pillars – A Leader's Manual
Come Higher Friends (The Interior Life Explained)
Prepare the Way of the Lord (Inner Healing)
Sound the Trumpet
Your Kingdom Come
Fires of Hope

Multi-media Series

The Power of Intercessory Prayer
Contemplative Spirituality
Desert Briefings
Powers and Principalities
International Conference on Intercessory Prayer &
Spiritual Warfare
Church Alive
Bridges
The Lamb
Wings

Family Formation Series

Family Formation I and II
A Teaching Series for the entire family
Teach your children the charism of Contemplative and
Intercessory Prayer.
Learn while you teach.
It includes a disk of handouts and worksheets for children.

Family Formation III
A Teaching Series for the entire family
that focuses on discovering the Seven Capital Sins.
It includes concrete, hands-on exercises and examples for
the whole family and a disk of handouts and worksheet for
children.

Family Formation IV
A Teaching Series for the entire family
on the stages of the Interior Life.

It includes clear and easy to understand teachings on the stages of spiritual growth and a disk of handouts and worksheets for children.

View our online catalog at www.bellwetheromaha.org.

Translations of selected materials are available in several languages.
Contact the Intercessors of the Lamb for details.

Some materials are also available in digital format.